BLUEPRINT FOR WORLD CONQUEST

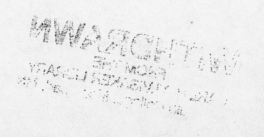

Blueprint for World Conquest

AS OUTLINED BY
THE COMMUNIST INTERNATIONAL

With an Introduction by
WILLIAM HENRY CHAMBERLIN

Human Events
WASHINGTON·CHICAGO
1946

When, in the Course of human events . . .
THE DECLARATION OF INDEPENDENCE, 1776

PUBLISHERS NOTE

I T HAS BEEN FREQUENTLY ASSERTED within the last few months that the peace of the world depends on the orderly co-operation of the United States and the Soviet Union. The American people have also been often admonished that our difficulties with the Soviet Union arise from our lack of understanding of the Russian point of view. The publication of the documents contained in this book was undertaken so that the American people might have the opportunity of learning Russia's aims from an unimpeachable source—the official documents of the Communist International, headquarters in Moscow.

The documents printed in this book are reproduced exactly and in their entirety from the following sources:

The Theses and Statutes of the Communist International [as adopted at the Second World Congress, July 17 to August 7, 1920 at Moscow, Russia] (New York: Central Executive Committee of the Communist Party of America, 1921).

"Constitution and Rules of the Communist International," *International Press Correspondence*, Volume VIII Number 84, November 28, 1928.

"The Programme of the Communist International," Adopted by the Sixth World Congress on September 1st, 1928 in Moscow, *International Press Correspondence* (Vienna), Volume VIII Number 92, December 31, 1928.

The blue lines printed in the margins opposite certain parts of the Theses and Statutes and the Programme of the Communist International are intended to set off the most important passages.

The spelling has been Americanized in the last two documents.

CONTENTS

☭

PART 1

INTRODUCTION   1

PART 2

THE THESES AND STATUTES
OF THE COMMUNIST INTERNATIONAL   29

PART 3

PROGRAM OF THE
COMMUNIST INTERNATIONAL   147

PART 4

CONSTITUTION AND RULES
OF THE COMMUNIST INTERNATIONAL   247

PART 1
INTRODUCTION

INTRODUCTION

THE REPRINTING OF THESE DOCUMENTS which set forth with complete authority and with remarkable detail the technique by means of which Communism hopes to conquer the world is a great and badly needed public service. The threat of Communism, which is now primarily a fifth column agency of Soviet Russian infiltration and expansion, to the peace and stability of the world is infinitely greater than it was in 1920 or in 1928, when these blueprints of international conspiracy were composed.

For in 1920 Russia was a land so torn by civil strife, so weakened by social and economic upheaval, that it was unable to give effective physical assistance to revolutionary movements outside its own borders. The will to give such assistance was certainly not lacking. The present Soviet policy of imposing on Poland a Communist-dominated puppet government was foreshadowed in 1920, when the Soviet Government refused favorable peace proposals and staked everything on capturing Warsaw and setting up a Soviet regime in Poland. But this attempt failed because the Red Army was decisively defeated in the battle before Warsaw.

Physical conditions in Russia had improved in 1928, by comparison with the bleak picture of hunger, cold, decline of agriculture and virtual prostration of industry which prevailed in 1920. But the country was still in no condition to undertake a major war of aggression. Com-

1

munist agents, to be sure, played a considerable role in stirring up riots, strikes, rebellions and civil conflict all the way from China to Bulgaria. But the Soviet Government could not with any safety or discretion throw the weight of the Red Army into the scales.

Soviet military weakness furnishes the true explanation of Litvinov's hypocritical pleas for disarmament, peace and collective security which made such an impression on gullible public opinion in America and other foreign countries. How hypocritical these pleas must seem, in the light of the iron dogmas of Communist philosophy, will be evident to anyone who reads these documents, with their constant, repeated emphasis on the necessity for international and civil war as a prelude to the final triumph of Communism throughout the world.

It is obvious that any government whose leaders are animated by this philosophy could only be super-militarist in character. If war is inevitable, and this proposition is advanced over and over again, it would be sheer imbecility not to make every conceivable political, economic, military and psychological preparation to win. And here one finds the perfect clue to Soviet policy before World War II, during World War II, and since World War II.

Now, the balance of international force has changed appreciably in favor of the Soviet Union. Despite heavy losses in manpower and industrial equipment, the Soviet Union is an unchallenged member of the Big Three. It is far and away the strongest land Power in Europe and in Asia, in terms of area, population, natural resources, armaments and trained military forces.

Events have already shown that it proposes to use its new strength without the slightest regard for its own voluntarily assumed treaty obligations or for the idealistic phrases which were inserted into the Charter of the United Nations. The Soviet diplomatic record is a shambles of broken treaties and obligations. The non-aggression treaties which the Soviet Government concluded, at its own initiative, with Poland, Finland, Latvia, Lithuania and Estonia were all treated as scraps of paper at the first convenient opportunity.

The non-aggression treaty with Japan was broken as soon as the Soviet Government saw an opportunity to gain cheap spoils in Manchuria and Korea after Japan's collapse was assured. Soviet promises at Yalta to insure "free and unfettered elections" in Poland have already been dishonored over and over again by the institution in occupied Poland of a government whose key figures (Bierut, Gomolka, Radkiewicz, Berman) are not only Communists, but indoctrinated and trained Moscow agents. Equally obvious is the disregard, in Romania, Bulgaria and Yugoslavia, of the Yalta promise that the Soviet Union, the United States and Great Britain will jointly assist the peoples in liberated States "to form interim governmental authorities broadly representative of all democratic elements in the population and pledged to the earliest possible establishment through free elections of governments responsive to the will of the people."

Just how this promise has been carried out in practice may be judged from the following excerpt from a dispatch of R. H. Markham, experienced correspondent of

3

the *Christian Science Monitor* in Bulgaria, in the *Monitor* for October 6, 1945:

> "Bulgarian Communists are heavily armed, while all other Bulgarians are disarmed. The Bulgarian militia, which is exclusively in the hands of the Communists, is master in every village and city. Many concentration camps are maintained for political opponents, and any Bulgarian citizen at any time may be seized and sent to such camps in utter disregard of the courts—and kept there as long as the Communist Party wishes. There is not a single city in Bulgaria or many villages where citizens have not been tortured or killed by irresponsible elements connected with the régime."

In the early Thirties Stalin announced as a government policy:

> "We shall not yield an inch of our own soil, we do not want a foot of anyone else's."

This statement deserves to rank with some of Hitler's assurances that this or that demand was positively his last. Stalin, it may be noted, did not say:

> We do not want a foot of foreign soil, except Latvia, Lithuania, Estonia, Eastern Poland, parts of Finland, Bessarabia, Northern Bukovina, Eastern Czechoslovakia, Persian Azerbaijan, etc., etc.

Public opinion is sometimes curiously illogical in its reactions. There was undoubtedly more apprehension of the threat of Communism after the First World War, when Russia was quite helpless to undertake major military operations outside its own borders, than there is now, when the Soviet Union is one of the world's great military powers.

4

This is partly the result of the hangover of the propaganda during the war, when all unfavorable references to the Soviet system and philosophy were officially discouraged. There has also been a big softening-up campaign, launched from Communist and near-Communist sources and designed to induce the American people to take an ostrich attitude toward the plain facts of Soviet aggression and expansion in defiance of treaty obligations and the principles of the Atlantic Charter, of which the Soviet Union is a co-signatory.

Curiously enough this campaign is often spearheaded by individuals who formerly insisted that appeasement of or compromise with Hitler and the Japanese militarists was at once futile and dishonorable. They now devote their energies to trying to prove that appeasement of the Soviet dictatorship, sacrifice of one free people after another to its expansionist claims, is both honorable and enlightened.

The success of this campaign among supposedly independent publications, opinion-forming groups and agencies is disquieting. The most strained, irrelevant and sometimes palpably absurd arguments are used to lull American apprehension about the obvious fact of extensive Soviet aggressive expansion far beyond the frontiers with which Soviet leaders repeatedly professed full satisfaction before 1939. Russia, we are told, needs "security" and is therefore presumably entitled to destroy the security and independence of its weaker neighbors.

The falsity of this contention lies in the fact that aggression can never make for genuine security, unless it is prosecuted to the ultimate point of conquest of the

5

entire globe. In an age of atomic bombs and air warfare, strips of 100 or 200 miles of foreign territory are entirely without significance from the standpoint of national defense.

Recent Soviet aggression against Iran in violation of the Anglo-Soviet-American agreement to respect the independence and territorial integrity of that country is sometimes justified on the ground that the Soviet Union needs Iranian oil, although Soviet geologists have long been boasting that their country contains some of the richest oil deposits in the world. As a variation on this theme it is suggested that the Iranian Government is corrupt and undesirable anyway. Indeed it is noteworthy how quickly any government which desires to preserve the independence of its people from Soviet aggression, whether it be the Chinese, the Polish, the Finnish, the Greek, the Turkish, is quickly characterized as "reactionary," "feudal," "anti-democratic," perhaps "fascist."

Promoters of the softening-up appeasement campaign in this country often put forward as an excuse for any and every case of Soviet breach-of-contract and assault-and-battery in the international sphere that Russia is "suspicious" of the outside world. That this Soviet attitude is fully justified is simply taken for granted, even though the democratic Powers which are the principal objects of suspicion saved the Soviet Union from overwhelming defeat in the late war.

On the other hand, suspicion of Soviet actions and intentions, however well grounded in fact, is treated as something akin to treason or fascism. It is naively assumed that if disagreeable realities are never mentioned

6

their consequences will not be felt.

In the atmosphere of ignorant unreality which dominates much thinking and speaking about Russia, it is
extremely valuable to place before thoughtful Americans
a summary of the philosophy which dominates the thinking of Stalin and other Soviet leaders. There can be no
question as to the authority and authenticity of the documents reprinted here.[1]

One is a statement of the resolutions and theoretical
instructions drawn up at the Second Congress of the
Communist International, held in Moscow from July 17
until August 7, 1920. The others contain similar material, prepared at the Sixth Congress of the International
in Moscow in 1928.

We have the testimony of the veteran Communist,
D. Z. Manuilsky, who represented the Ukrainian Soviet
Republic at the San Francisco Conference and at the
opening session of U N in London, that "not one important document of big international significance was
issued by the Communist International without the most
active participation of Comrade Stalin in its composition."[2]

The fact that the Communist International formally
dissolved itself in the spring of 1943 does not affect the
validity of the working program of revolutionary action

---

[1] *The Theses and Statutes of the Communist International*, as adopted by
the Second World Congress, July 17 to August 7, 1920; *Constitution and
Rules of the Communist International*, as adopted by the Sixth World
Congress, September 1, 1928; *The Program of the Communist International*, as adopted by the Sixth World Congress, September 1, 1928.

[2] See *Stalin*, a publication in Russian of reminiscences and laudatory tributes,
issued by OGIZ, the Soviet State Publishing House, p. 93.

7

which Stalin helped to prepare. In the first place, there is no evidence that Communist parties outside of Russia have ceased to keep time by the Kremlin clock since the International was outwardly disbanded. In the second place, Stalin is a single, not a dual, personality. The doctrines which he actively participated in formulating, as a leader of the Communist International, inevitably affect his thinking and his actions as the dictatorial chief of a powerful State.

That he would not express such views to foreign diplomats, businessmen and journalists is rather obvious, especially when one finds in the documents repeated instructions pointing to various forms of deceit and camouflage essential to the pursuit of the goal of world revolution. In politics, as in war, the clever strategist tries to conceal his true objective.

So an inaccurate and oversimplified interpretation of Russian development since the Revolution has been cleverly sold to credulous foreigners and passed on to soothe American public opinion. It is represented that Trotsky was a bad man who wanted to incite revolution all over the world, while Stalin was a good man who merely wished to build up Russia's national power and resources.

But the truth of the matter is that Stalin is just as much committed to the ultimate objective of world revolution through the overthrow of all "capitalist" States as was Trotsky. Apart from the personal rivalry between these two heirs of Lenin, the difference was not as to the end, but as to the means by which this end could best be achieved.

8

Trotsky, the theorist, the agitator, the doctrinaire, clung to the old-fashioned orthodox method of trying to stir up working class revolutions in countries outside of Russia.

Stalin, more practical, more cynical, more opportunist, drew certain lessons from the failure of the Communist International to win any important victories during the first years of its existence. So he concentrated his attention on building up Russia as a mighty totalitarian militarist State which could impose Soviet political and economic changes on weaker neighbors at the first convenient opportunity. At the same time he kept a tight rein on Communist parties throughout the world as useful agencies of volunteer propaganda and espionage in normal times, as potential fifth column auxiliaries prepared to commit treason and sabotage when the day of advancing world conquest should arrive.

The belief that Stalin has renounced interest in revolution outside of Russia can be disproved by his own words. His book *Leninism*, while it is drier and less lurid in style, is just as much a "must" for Soviet youth as Hitler's *Mein Kampf* was for the Nazi younger generation in Germany. And this is what Stalin wrote in the 1933 edition of *Leninism*:

"The victory of socialism in one country is not an end in itself; it must be looked upon as a support, as a means for hastening the proletarian victory in every other land. For the victory of the revolution in one country (in Russia, for the nonce) is not only the result of the unequal development and the progressive decay of imperialism; it is likewise the beginning and

9

the continuation of the world revolution."[3]

Equally revealing is Stalin's official explanation of the reason for maintaining in Russia the terrorist political police, formerly known as the G P U, more recently as the N K V D. Talking to a French Workers delegation in 1927, he said:

> "From the point of view of the internal situation, the revolution is so firm and unshakable that we could do without the GPU. But the trouble is that the enemies at home are not isolated individuals. They are connected in a thousand ways with the capitalists of all countries who support them by every means and in every way. We are a country surrounded by capitalist states. The internal enemies of our revolution are the agents of the capitalists of *all* [author's italics] countries."[4]

What does this mean? It means that in Stalin's mind there is irreconcilable hostility between the Soviet Union and the "capitalist" world. It means that Russia can never know security so long as "capitalist" (i.e., democratic) States continue to exist.

A man publicly committed to such ideas would only be acting logically if he set as his aim the elimination of the "capitalist" States which he regards as irreconcilably hostile. And here Stalin's ambitions are clearly reflected in the course of events during and since the Second World War. Twelve formerly independent States in Eastern Europe (Poland, Latvia, Lithuania, Estonia, Finland, Czechoslovakia, Yugoslavia, Bulgaria, Romania,

[3] J. Stalin, *Leninism* (London: Allen & Unwin, 1933), I, 212.
[4] *Ibid.*, II, 91.

Hungary, Austria, Albania) have been brought under some form of Soviet control. The type of this control varies from the outright annexation which has been imposed on the Baltic States and Eastern Poland to the more indirect, remote control system which prevails in Finland and Czechoslovakia, Austria and Hungary. In between these two extremes are the puppet regimes, with all strings pulled from Moscow, which have been set up in Poland and Romania, Bulgaria and Yugoslavia. Soviet troops are also in occupation of a large part of Germany and of the Danish island of Bornholm, key to the southern approach to Sweden.

Soviet occupation is sometimes referred to, with unconscious irony, as "liberation." Actually it is only the substitution of one tyranny for another, of one type of Quisling regime for another. Moscow time, literally as well as figuratively, has been substituted for Berlin time over a great area of Eastern Europe. This area, inhabited by more than one hundred million human beings and possessing a varied wealth of natural resources, has been directly or indirectly annexed to the Soviet Union, which contained within its borders between one sixth and one seventh of the land surface of the globe and a population of about one hundred and seventy million people before the outbreak of the Second World War.

Winston Churchill once referred to Soviet foreign policy as "a riddle wrapped in a mystery inside an enigma." This same idea must have frequently occurred to puzzled and well-meaning Americans as they surveyed the yawning gap between what they would like to believe about their wartime ally, the Soviet Union, and the actions and policies of the Soviet Government.

Here was a country which professed the desire only to build up its new social and economic order peacefully within its own frontiers. Not one American in a million would challenge the right of the Soviet peoples to maintain any political, economic or social system they might prefer, however different from our own this might be. But this professed desire for peaceful development within its own very ample pre-1939 frontiers has been discredited again by arbitrary seizures of foreign territory and violent imposition of puppet regimes.

Here was a country which, as Americans heard and liked to believe, was committed to the ideal of free and frank cooperation with its wartime allies in the interest of a new stable world order based on justice. Yet Soviet policy remained as furtive and secretive in its methods, as violent and unilateral in its actions, as ever. Promises were made only to be broken; treaties were concluded only to be disregarded. Whereas democratic countries lifted censorship after the end of hostilities, Soviet censorship remained in full force. There was no apparent disposition to eliminate the obstacles to free travel and uninhibited reporting of Soviet conditions.

Soviet propagandists tried to make capital out of Soviet disarmament proposals in the Twenties, out of Litvinov's speeches in favor of the principle of collective security in the Thirties. But these were voices of the past. One looks in vain to Moscow now for any lead in the direction of limitation of armaments or genuine collective security. More than a third of the Soviet budget after the end of the war was devoted to military purposes. Instead of sup-

12

porting proposals for world order based on law and justice, the Soviet Government exercised all its influence to insure the right of every Great Power to veto any action by the United Nations directed against aggression. Soviet diplomats and journalists exalted Big Three Unity, rather than collective security as an ideal. And they interpreted Big Three Unity as meaning that Russia should have its way on every disputed international question.

What is the clue to these puzzling contradictions, the solution of the Soviet riddle? I think the thoughtful reader will find important light in these documents, where the basic principles of Soviet Communism, its assumptions of international action, are set forth in the clearest and most unequivocal form. Here one has the Soviet equivalent of Hitler's *Mein Kampf*, the Soviet version of the "Tanaka Memorial," in which that Japanese militarist drew up his blueprint for the subjugation of East Asia and ultimately of the world.

It is to be hoped that American readers will not be diverted from close and careful study of this revealing material because the language is sometimes dry and abstruse and because some of the economic and philosophic dogmas seem extremely silly. The world would be much better off today if it had never tried to laugh off Adolf Hilter. With this precedent in mind, it would be unwise to brush aside as trivial or unimportant the amazing blueprint of world conquest through internal propaganda, division, subversion and treason which is unfolded in such minute detail. It would be more sensible to reflect on how large a part of the Communist dream of world conquest is already a reality.

13

Many of the unruly pieces in the jigsaw puzzle of Soviet foreign policy fall neatly into place as one follows attentively the short-range and long-range strategy outlined in these pronouncements of the high councils of the Communist faith. Why take U N seriously if wars between "capitalist" and Communist States are predestined and unavoidable? Why expect treaties and promises to be observed when deceit and camouflage are recommended as essential elements in the technique of Communist propaganda? For the same reason, why take seriously the professions of innocence of the numerous Communist "front" organizations which exist in America and other countries?

A valuable feature of these documents is their extreme frankness. There is no beating about the bush, no suggestion that Communists are just well-meaning liberal social reformers. The 21 conditions[5] which the Second Congress of the Communist International laid down for parties desiring to affiliate with this organization represent the most complete school for treason which could very well be imagined.

Communist parties are instructed "to create everywhere a parallel illegal apparatus," to combine "legal" and "illegal" work. Misguided Americans who, in the name of a false conception of civil liberty, maintain that Communists should be eligible for commissions in the armed forces should consider the implications of Condition 4, which reads literally as follows:

"Persistent and systematic propaganda and agitation must be carried on in the army, where Communist

[5]Pp. 65 ff.

14

groups should be formed in every military organization. Wherever owing to repressive legislation agitation becomes impossible, it is necessary to carry on such agitation illegally. But refusal to carry on or participate in such work should be considered equal to treason to the revolutionary cause, and incompatible with affiliation to the Third International."

Suppose a Communist in uniform obtained access to some important military secret. Is there the slightest doubt that he would turn it over to the Soviet Union at the first opportunity? In view of this circumstance it is just as reasonable to bar Communists from responsible posts in the armed forces as it would be to keep agents of foreign intelligence services out of our military and industrial establishments.

Those who believe that the Soviet Government is genuinely interested in seeing U N function effectively may be referred to Condition 6:

"Every party desirous of affiliating to the Third International should renounce not only avowed social patriotism, but also the falsehood and the hypocrisy of social pacifism: it should systematically demonstrate to the workers that without a revolutionary overthrow of capitalism no international arbitration, no talk of disarmament, no democratic reorganization of the League of Nations will be capable of saving mankind from new imperialist wars."

Is it surprising that some trade-unions and "cultural" organizations in which Communist tactics of infiltration have been successful should invariably take sides with Russia and against America when one reads the ninth of the 21 conditions:

"Every party desirous of belonging to the Communist International should be bound to carry on systematic and persistent Communist work in the labor unions, co-operatives and other organizations of working masses. It is necessary to form Communist nuclei within these organizations, which by persistent and lasting work should win over labor unions to communism."

Condition 14 is illuminating as to the obligation of the Communist to fight for Russia against his own country in the event of any conflict:

"Each party desirous of affiliating to the Communist International should be obliged to render every possible assistance to the Soviet Republics in their struggle against all counter-revolutionary forces. The Communist parties should carry on a precise and definite propaganda to induce the workers to refuse to transport any kind of military equipment intended for fighting against the Soviet Republics, and should also by legal or illegal means carry on a propaganda amongst the troops sent against the workers' republics, etc."

Very often the wording of these Communist resolutions is a preview of events which were to occur in the future. Stirring up revolution in China and India was recognized as "one of the most important questions before the Second Congress of the Third International." How is this objective to be realized? A tortuous and complicated strategy is outlined in the following excerpts from the resolution on this question:

"It is the duty of the Communist International to support the revolutionary movement in the colonies and in the backward countries, . . . The Communist

International must establish temporary relations and even unions with the revolutionary movements in the colonies and backward countries, without however amalgamating with them, but preserving the independent character of the proletarian movement even though it be still in its embryonic state. . . .

"The revolution in the colonies is not going to be a Communist revolution in its first stages. But if from the outset the leadership is in the hands of a Communist vanguard, the revolutionary masses will not be led astray, but may go ahead through the successive periods of development of revolutionary experience...."[6]

The phraseology is dry and complex. But the meaning is clear. Communists are to enter nationalist movements, like the Chinese Kuomintang, the Indian National Congress, etc., go along with these movements in their struggle against "foreign imperialism," but retain their independent organization, so that they may seize the reins of power at the first convenient opportunity.

This is a precise blueprint of the strategy which the Chinese Communists, constantly coached by their Soviet advisers, followed in China during the Twenties. Because Chiang Kai-shek frustrated their maneuver and drove them out of the Kuomintang in the decisive year, 1927, the Generalissimo has been the object of the unrelenting hatred and vilification of Communists and fellow-travellers all over the world. However much one may hope for Chinese unity and cessation of civil strife, it remains to be seen what use the Chinese Communists will make of the offices which they will presumably hold

[6]Pp. 124-125, 130.

if a coalition government is finally organized in China.

When Winston Churchill's predominantly Conservative Government gave way to a Labor Cabinet in Great Britain last summer some naive commentators believed that a honeymoon era in Soviet-British relations was in prospect. But democratic socialism is one of the principal hates of dictatorial Communism. Democratic socialist parties were outlawed in Russia under the Soviet regime. Their members were killed, sent to concentration camps or driven into exile. Two of the most prominent Polish Social Democrats, Henryk Ehrlich and Viktor Alter, were shot after the first Soviet occupation of Poland. The sharp exchanges which have marked some of the meetings of the British Foreign Minister, Ernest Bevin, with Molotov, Vishinsky and other Soviet representatives were foreshadowed in the following vituperative references to moderate socialists and labor leaders in the resolutions of the Sixth Congress of the Communist International:

"A cynically commercial, and imperialistic secular form of subjecting the proletariat to the ideological influence of the bourgeoisie is represented by contemporary 'socialist' reformism. Taking its main gospel from the tablets of imperialist politics, its model today is the deliberately anti-socialist and openly counter-revolutionary 'American Federation of Labor'. The 'ideological' dictatorship of the servile American trade union bureaucracy, which in its turn expresses the 'ideological' dictatorship of the American dollar, has become, through the medium of British reformism and His Majesty's Socialists of the British Labor Party, the

18

most important constituent in the theory and practice of international Social Democracy . . .

". . . Social Democracy has utterly and completely betrayed Marxism, having traversed the road from revisionism to complete liberal bourgeois reformism and avowed social-imperialism: it has substituted in place of the Marxian theory of the contradiction of capitalism, the bourgeois theory of its harmonious development; it has pigeonholed the theory of crisis and of the pauperization of the proletariat; it has turned the flaming and menacing theory of class struggle into prosaic advocacy of class peace . . . in place of the theory of the inevitability of war under capitalism it has substituted the bourgeois deceit of pacifism . . . It has replaced revolution by evolution, the destruction of the bourgeois State by its active upbuilding . . ."[7]

In this diatribe, as in much Communist polemical literature, it is noteworthy that there are two unforgivable sins. One is belief in the possibility of permanent peace under "capitalism." The other is to suggest that social grievances can be redressed and social tensions relaxed by a process of orderly and peaceful progress within the framework of a democratic political system.

Not the possibility or probability, but the *inevitability* of wars between nations and of violent "proletarian" revolution throughout the world is stressed over and over again with such dogmatic finality that one can only reasonably assume that these convictions are firmly held by all prominent Communists, including the leaders of the Soviet Union. Take, for example, the following sentence in the introduction to the Program and resolutions

[7]Pp. 225, 227.

19

adopted at the Sixth Congress of the Communist International, in 1928:

"... With elemental force, imperialism exposes and accentuates all the contradictions of capitalist society; it carries class oppression to the utmost limits, intensifies the struggle between capitalist governments, *inevitably* [author's italics] gives rise to world-wide imperialist wars that shake the whole prevailing system of relationships to their foundations and *inexorably* [author's italics] leads to the World Proletarian Revolution."[8]

No thoughtful person, after reading *Mein Kampf*, with its frequent insistence on the necessity of war, could have felt that world peace would be very secure once the author of this work had become master of the most powerful military and industrial State in Europe. For just the same reasons the outlook for future world peace is not improved by the fact that the dictatorial leaders of one of the world's three most powerful States are so deeply indoctrinated with the ideas that war and violent revolution are inescapable phases of the historical process.

We learn from these official documents that profound deceit and hypocrisy are required of Communists as a duty to the cause. The frequent repudiation by Communists of their membership in the party, the familiar trick, in America, of forming organizations under Communist control with innocent sounding labels—"liberal," "constitutional liberties," "democratic," "progressive," "anti-fascist," etc.—acquire new significance in the light of the following instructions to Communists throughout

[8]P. 149.

the world. These are quoted verbatim:

". . . It is especially necessary to carry on illegal work in the army, navy and police . . .

"On the other hand, it is also necessary in all cases without exception not to limit oneself to illegal work, but to carry on also legal work overcoming all difficulties, founding a legal press and legal organizations under the most diverse circumstances, and in case of need, frequently changing names. . . .

". . . the Communist parties must create a new type of periodical press for extensive circulation among the workmen: 1) Legal publications, in which the Communists *without calling themselves such and without mentioning their connection with the party* [author's italics], would learn to utilize the slightest possibility allowed by the laws as the Bolsheviki did at the time of the Tzar, after 1905.

"2) Illegal sheets, although of the smallest dimensions and irregularly published, but reproduced in most of the printing offices by workmen (in secret, or if the movement has grown stronger, by means of a revolutionary seizure of the printing offices), and giving the proletariat undiluted revolutionary information and the revolutionary slogans."[9]

This is followed by a glint of unconscious humor in the shape of the statement:

"Without involving the masses in the revolutionary struggle for a free Communist press the preparation for the dictatorship of the proletariat is impossible."[10]

In other words, the masses are to be incited, in the name of freedom of the Communist press, to set up a

[9]Pp. 54, 55, 56.   [10]P. 56.

21

regime in which there will be no freedom for any kind of press.

It is quite obvious from our American experience that the instructions about creating camouflaged organs of opinion, directed in the Communist spirit without admitting any connection with the Communist party, has been followed on a very wide scale. It is equally obvious that individuals who have been taught to lie and cheat, to conceal their true opinions, to practice hypocrisy as a matter of party discipline, are excellently conditioned for espionage and fifth column work.

The most important function of Communist parties outside of Russia is this fifth column activity, which varies from country to country, depending on the strength of the Communist movement and the immediate needs of Soviet foreign policy. In those countries and regions which have been annexed by the Soviet Union or which are politically controlled from Moscow (Latvia, Lithuania, Estonia, Poland, Yugoslavia, Bulgaria, Romania, etc.) the Communists, especially those who have gone through long indoctrination training in special schools in Moscow, supply the key men in the local puppet regimes.

In lands where the Communists possess a strong mass following, but do not yet feel able to take over power (France, for instance) they constantly put pressure on the government to follow a pro-Soviet line in foreign policy. How strictly the Communist deputies in any parliament or congress are controlled by the party organization may be judged from the wording of Condition 11 laid down for parties which desire to join the Communist International:

> "Parties desirous of joining the Third International shall be bound to inspect the personnel of their parliamentary factions, to remove all unreliable elements therefrom, to control such factions, not only verbally but in reality, to subordinate them to the Central Committee of the party, and to demand from each Communist representative in parliament to subject his entire activity to the interests of real revolutionary propaganda, and agitation."[11]

Finally there remain countries like the United States and Great Britain, Canada and Australia, Sweden and Switzerland, where deep-rooted traditions of democracy and liberty and a relatively high standard of living have greatly restricted the appeal of Communism. In such countries the Communists are not numerous enough to elect many representatives to national and local legislative bodies. But they are by no means useless to their Moscow masters. Because of their tight discipline and their experience in conspiratorial technique, they wield an influence out of all proportion to their numbers. A few Communists, knowing what they want and working closely together, can often infiltrate into key positions in a trade-union, a so-called cultural organization, a government agency.

Any doubt as to the close association of the Soviet regime with revolutionary movements in other countries, with insurgent colonial movements, should be cleared up by the following statements in the resolutions of the Sixth Congress of the Communist International:

[11]P. 69.

23

". . . the U. S. S. R. inevitably becomes the base of the world movement of all oppressed classes, *the center of international revolution* [author's italics] the greatest factor in world history. In the U. S. S. R., the world proletariat for the first time acquires a country that is really its own, and for the colonial movements the U. S. S. R. becomes a powerful center of attraction. . . .

"The systematic imperialist attempts politically to encircle the U. S. S. R. and the growing danger of an armed attack upon her, do not, however, prevent the Communist Party of the Soviet Union—a section of the Communist International and the leader of the proletarian dictatorship in the U. S. S. R.—from fulfilling its international obligations and from rendering support to all the oppressed, to the labor movements in capitalist countries, to colonial movements against imperialism and to the struggle against national oppression in every form."[12]

This affords a fair gauge of the sincerity of the professions of lack of interest in subversive movements outside of Russia which Stalin and other Soviet leaders have periodically voiced to credulous visitors who were usually very imperfectly familiar with the basic doctrines of Communism. The argument that the Communist Party in Russia could take an active part in the work of the Communist International without involving the Soviet Government is quite absurd, since the leaders of the Party and of the Soviet Government form a close interlocking directorate.

So much for the "international obligations" of the Communist Party in the U. S. S. R. to assist revolution-

[12]Pp. 220, 222.

24

ary movements throughout the world. The corresponding obligation of foreign Communists to act as a fifth column for the Soviet Union is equally clearly defined as follows:

". . . the international proletariat must on its part facilitate the success of the work of Socialist construction in the U. S. S. R. and defend her against the attacks of the capitalist powers by all the means in its power. . . .

"In the event of the imperialist States declaring war upon and attacking the U. S. S. R., the international proletariat must retaliate by organizing bold and determined mass action and struggle for the overthrow of the imperialist governments with the slogan of: Dictatorship of the proletariat and alliance with the U. S. S. R. . . .

"Thus, the development of the contradictions within modern world economy, the development of the general capitalist crisis, and the imperialist military attack upon the Soviet Union inevitably lead to a mighty revolutionary outbreak which must overwhelm capitalism in a number of the so-called civilized countries, unleash the victorious revolution in the colonies, broaden the base of the proletarian dictatorship to an enormous degree and thus, with tremendous strides, bring nearer the final world victory of Socialism."[13]

This lends new significance to the characterization of the United States Government as "the enemy" by Joseph Starobin in the Communist newspaper, "The Daily Worker," of January 2, 1946.

There are many more interesting and illuminating passages in these authoritative blueprints of the Com-

[13]Pp. 222, 223.

25

munist scheme for world conquest. A technique of subversion is outlined for every nation, for every class, for every type of political situation.

Inasmuch as the philosophy outlined in these documents dominates the thinking of the rulers of one of the strongest military Powers in the world, American readers should become familiar with it. They can find here the explanation of many Soviet methods and actions which would seem ill-advised, even irrational, on the part of a regime which was sincerely anxious to cultivate international peace and good-will.

The publication of these documents will doubtless excite in Communist and fellow-traveller circles the familiar outcries, "redbaiter," "Russophobe," "Russiahater" with which these circles try to stifle any serious and objective discussion of the Soviet regime and its foreign policies. But at least another familiar phrase about "sowing suspicion" can scarcely find much application in this case. For the documents were originally published under the imprimatur of the highest Communist authority. They are not the speculations of a "suspicious" foreign observer, but the considered judgments of Lenin, Trotsky, Zinoviev, Bukharin, Stalin, Manuilsky and other Soviet Communist leaders, alive and dead.

The Communist International was dissolved as a tactical maneuver. But the militant revolutionary philosophy set forth in these documents has never been repudiated. It has been inculcated in the Russian younger generation which has grown up under Soviet influence. It will be extended to the countries which have fallen under Soviet control, where the Ministries of Education, like the Ministries of the Interior (Police), have been almost invariably placed in the hands of Communists.

The contents of these documents should be known to every member of Congress, to every official of the United States Government, to every diplomat, to everyone who is concerned with shaping American relations with the U. S. S. R. The significance of these documents should be carefully weighed in considering various aspects of American-Soviet relations.

One may hope that this fantastic scheme of world conquest through revolution will be abandoned. But until there is convincing proof that the Soviet Government has given up the desire to expand aggressively beyond its proper frontiers (and so far there has unfortunately been no such proof), the only sensible attitude of the United States and other democratic countries toward the blueprint of organized subversion which is outlined in these documents is to maintain the eternal vigilance that in this age, perhaps more than ever, is the price of liberty.

WILLIAM HENRY CHAMBERLIN

PART 2

THE THESES AND STATUTES
OF THE COMMUNIST INTERNATIONAL

As Adopted at the Second World Congress,
July 17 to August 7, 1920, Moscow

PREFACE TO AMERICAN EDITION

THE THESES AND STATUTES of the Communist International as adopted by the Second World Congress, July 17th–August 7th, 1920, were received by the Communist Party of America in December, 1920, from the Publishing Office of the Communist International at Moscow. Upon examination of this edition, which was translated into English in Moscow, it was found to contain many errors which led the Editorial Committee of the Communist Party to make a careful analysis of the text. It was compared with the German edition and the original Russian text with the result that many omissions and distortions were discovered, and these were of such a nature as to make the Moscow English edition misleading.

For example: The last sentence of Paragraph 9 of the Statutes of the Communist International (page 7) of the Moscow edition reads as follows: "In the event of necessity the Executive Committee organizes in various countries its technical and auxiliary bureaux, which are entirely under the control of the Executive Committee." The correct rendering of this passage should read (after the word "bureaux") ". . . completely subordinated to the Executive Committee. These representatives of the Executive Committee shall carry out their political tasks in closest contact with the Central Committee of the Communist Party of a given country."

In the Theses on "The Fundamental Tasks of the Communist International," Paragraph 5 (page 13) reads, ". . . But it follows from the above that the duty for the moment of the Communist Parties consists in accelerating the revolution, without provoking it artificially until sufficient preparation has been made; such preparation is to be carried on and emphasized by revolutionary activity.", whereas the sentence should read (after the word "consists"); ". . . not in accelerating the revolution, but in extensively preparing the proletariat for it." This same paragraph further speaks of ". . . a dictatorship of the groups and parties recognizing the dictatorship of the proletariat . . .", which is incorrect; and in Paragraph 7 (page 14) appears the statement that "the dictatorship of the proletariat—which will never be able to suppress completely all private ownership— . . .", whereas the clause should read; ". . . the dictatorship of the proletariat—which will never be able to destroy at once all private ownership—etc."

This edition of the Theses, which is published by the Central Executive Committee of the Communist Party of America (section of the Communist International) is the only English translation which is free from serious error and which conforms to the original as adopted by the Second World Congress of the Communist International.

February, 1921.

CENTRAL EXECUTIVE COMMITTEE OF THE
COMMUNIST PARTY OF AMERICA.

STATUTES
OF THE COMMUNIST INTERNATIONAL

IN THE YEAR 1864 the First International Workingmen's Association—the First International—was formed in London. In the constitution of this International Workingmen's Association it was stated:

That the emancipation of the working class is to be attained by the working class itself.

That the struggle for the emancipation of the working class does not mean a struggle for class privileges and monopolies but a struggle for equal rights and equal obligations, for the abolition of every kind of class-domination.

That the economic subjection of the worker to the monopolists of the means of production, i.e., of the sources of life is the cause of enslavement in all its forms, the cause of all social misery, all moral degradation and political subordination.

That the economic emancipation of the working class is therefore the great aim which every political movement must be subordinated to.

That all attempts to attain this great aim have failed as yet because of the lack of solidarity between the workers in the different industries of each country, and the absence of the fraternal union between the working class of the different countries.

That the emancipation is neither a local nor a national problem but a problem of a social character embracing every civilized country, and the solution of which depends on the theoretical and practical co-operation of the most progressive countries.

That the present simultaneous revival of the workers'
movement in the industrial countries of Europe on the one
hand awakens new hopes whilst on the other hand it is a
solemn warning of the danger of relapse into the old errors
and an appeal for an immediate union of the hitherto
disconnected movement.

The Second International which was established in 1889
at Paris had undertaken to continue the work of the First
International. In 1914 at the outbreak of the world slaughter
it has suffered a complete collapse. Undermined by opportunism and damaged by the treason of its leaders who had
taken the side of the bourgeoisie—the Second International
perished.

The Third Communist International which has been
established in March, 1919, in the capital of the Russian
Socialist Federative Soviet Republic in the city of Moscow
solemnly proclaims before the entire world that it takes
upon itself to continue and to complete the great cause
begun by the First International Workers' Association.

The Third Communist International had been formed
at a moment when the imperialist slaughter of 1914–1918
in which the imperialist bourgeoisie of the various countries
had sacrificed twenty million men, came to an end.

Keep in mind the imperialist war! This is the first appeal
of the Communist International to every toiler wherever he
may live and whatever language he may speak. Keep in mind
that owing to the existence of the capitalist system a small
group of Imperialists had the opportunity during four long
years to compel the workers of various countries to cut each
other's throat. Keep in mind that the bourgeois war has cast
Europe and the entire world into a state of extreme destitu-
tion and starvation. Keep in mind that unless the capitalist
system is overthrown the repetition of such criminal war is

34

not only possible but inevitable.

In order to overthrow the international bourgeoisie and to create an international Soviet Republic as a transition stage to the complete abolition of the state, the Communist International will use all means at its disposal, including force of arms.

The Communist International considers the dictatorship of the proletariat as the only means for the liberation of humanity from the horrors of capitalism. The Communist International considers the Soviet form of government as the historically evolved form of this dictatorship of the proletariat.

The imperialist war is responsible for the close union of the fate of the workers of one country with the fate of the workers of all other countries. The imperialist war emphasizes once more what is pointed out in the statute of the First International: that the emancipation of labor is neither local, nor a national task, but one of an international character.

The Communist International once and forever breaks with the traditions of the Second International which in reality only recognized the white race. The Communist International makes it its task to emancipate the workers of the entire world. The ranks of the Communist International fraternally unite men of all colors: white, yellow and black— the toilers of the entire world.

The Communist International fully and unreservedly upholds the gains of the great proletarian revolution in Russia, the first victorious socialist revolution in the world's history, and calls upon all workers to follow the same road. The Communist International makes it its duty to support by all the power at its disposal every Soviet Republic wherever it may be formed.

The Communist International is aware that for the purpose of a speedy achievement of victory the International Association of workers which is struggling for the abolition of capitalism and the establishment of Communism should possess a firm and centralized organization. To all intents and purposes the Communist International should represent an universal Communist party, of which the parties operating in every country form individual sections. The apparatus of the Communist International is organized to secure to the toilers of every country the possibility at any given moment to obtain the maximum of aid from the organized workers of the other countries.

For this purpose the Communist International affirms the following items of its statute:

1. The new International Association of workers is established for the purpose of organizing common activity of the workers of various countries who are striving towards a single aim: the overthrow of capitalism, the establishment of the dictatorship of the proletariat and of the International Soviet Republic for the complete abolition of classes and the realization of socialism—this first step to Communist Society.

2. The new International Association of workers is called The Communist International.

3. All the parties and organizations comprising the Communist International bear the name of the Communist party of the given country (section of the Communist International).

4. The World Congress of all parties and organizations which form part of the Communist International is the supreme organ of this International. The World Congress as a rule convenes not less than once a year. The World Congress confirms the programs of the various parties com-

prising the Communist International. The World Congress discusses and decides the more important questions of program and tactics, which are connected with the activity of the Communist International. The number of decisive votes at the World Congress for every party and organization is decided upon by a special regulation of the Congress.

5. The World Congress elects an Executive Committee of the Communist International which serves as the leading organ of the Communist International in the intervals between the convention of World Congresses and is responsible only to the World Congress.

6. The residence of the Executive Committee of the Communist International is each time decided at the World Congress of the Communist International.

7. A special World Congress of the Communist International may be convened either by regulation of the Executive Committee, or at the demand of one half of the number of the parties which were part of the Communist International at the last World Congress.

8. The bulk of the work and responsibility in the Executive Committee of the Communist International lies with the party of that country where, in keeping with the regulation of the World Congress, the Executive Committee finds its residence at the time being. The party of the country in question sends to the Executive Committee not less than five members with a decisive vote. In addition to this one representative with a decisive vote is sent to the Communist International from ten to twelve of the largest of Communist parties. The list of these representatives is to be confirmed by the Universal Congress of the Communist International. The remaining parties and organizations forming part of the Communist International enjoy the right of sending to the Executive Committee one represent-

ative each with a consultative vote.

9. The Executive Committee is the leading organ of the Communist International during the conventions; the Executive Committee publishes in no less than four languages the central organ of the Communist International (the periodical "The Communist International"). The Executive Committee makes the necessary appeals on behalf of the Communist International, and issues instructions obligatory to all the parties and organizations which form part of the Communist International. The Executive Committee of the Communist International enjoys the right to demand from the affiliated parties the exclusion of groups of members who are guilty of the infringement of international proletarian discipline, as well as the exclusion from the Communist International of such parties guilty of the infringement of the regulations of the World Congress. These parties retain the right of appealing to the World Congress. In the event of necessity the Executive Committee organizes in various countries its technical and auxiliary bureaux, completely subordinated to the Executive Committee. The representatives of the Executive Committee shall carry out their political tasks in closest contact with the Central Committee of the Communist Party of the given country.

10. The Executive Committee of the Communist International enjoys the right to include in its ranks representatives of organizations and parties not affiliated with the Communist International but which are sympathetic towards Communism; these are to have a consultative vote only.

11. The organs of all the parties and organizations forming part of the Communist International as well as of those who are recognized sympathizers of the Communist Inter-

national are obliged to publish all official regulations of the Communist International and of its Executive Committee.

12. The general state of things in the whole of Europe and of America makes necessary for the Communists of the whole world an obligatory formation of illegal Communist organizations along with those existing legally. The Executive Committee shall be bound to see that this shall be carried out everywhere.

13. As a rule all political relations between the separate parties forming the Communist International are carried on through the Executive Committee of the Communist International. In cases of exigency direct relations are established, with the provision, however, that the Executive Committee of the Communist International is informed of the same at the same time.

14. The trade unions who have accepted the Communist platform and are united on an international scale under the control of the Executive Committee of the Communist International, form Trade Union Sections of the Communist International. The Communist Trade Unions send their representatives to the World Congresses of the Communist International through the medium of the Communist parties of their respective countries. Trade union sections of the Communist International delegate a representative with a decisive vote to the Executive Committee of the Communist International. The Executive Committee of the Communist International enjoys the right of sending a representative with decisive vote, to the Trade Union section of the Communist International.

15. The International League of Communist Youth is subject to the Communist International and its Executive Committee. One representative of the Executive Committee of the International League of Communist Youth

39

with a decisive vote is delegated to the Executive Committee of the Communist International. The Executive Committee of the Communist International, on the other hand, enjoys the right of sending a representative with a decisive vote to the executive organ of the International League of Communist Youth.

16. The Executive Committee of the Communist International confirms the International Secretary of the Communist Women's Movement and organizes a women's section of the Communist International.

17. In the event of a member of the Communist International coming to another country he is to have the fraternal support of the local members of the Third International.

THESES ADOPTED

BY THE SECOND CONGRESS

The Fundamental Tasks of the Communist International

A CHARACTERISTIC FEATURE of the present moment in the development of the international Communist movement, is the fact that in all the capitalist countries the best representatives of the revolutionary proletariat have completely understood the fundamental principles of the Communist International; namely, the dictatorship of the proletariat and the power of the Soviets, and with a loyal enthusiasm have placed themselves on the side of the Communist International. A still more important and great step forward is the unlimited sympathy with these principles manifested by the wider masses not only of the proletariat of the towns, but also by the advanced portion of the agrarian workers.

On the other hand two mistakes or weaknesses of the extraordinarily rapidly increasing international Communist movement have shown themselves. One, very serious and presenting a great direct danger for the success of the cause of the liberation of the proletariat, consists in the fact that part of the old leaders and old parties of the Second International, partly half unconsciously yielding to the wishes and pressure of the masses, partly consciously deceiving them in order to preserve their former role of agents and supporters of the bourgeoisie inside the labor movement, are declaring their conditional or even unconditional affiliation to the Third International; while remaining in reality in the whole practice of their party and political work, on the level of the Second International. Such a state of things is absolutely inadmissible, because it demoralizes the masses, hinders the development of a strong Communist Party, and lowers their respect for the Third International by threatening repetition of such betrayals as that of the Hungarian Social-Democrats, who had rapidly assumed the disguise of Communists. The second much less important mistake, which is, for the most part, a malady due to the rapid growth of the movement, is the tendency to be extremely "left," which leads to an erroneous valuation of the role and duties of the party in respect to the class and to the mass, and the obligation of the revolutionary Communists to work in the bourgeois parliaments and reactionary labor unions.

The duty of the Communists is not to gloss over any of the weaknesses of their movement, but to criticize them openly in order to get rid of them promptly and radically. To this end it is necessary, 1) to establish concretely, especially on the basis of the already acquired practical experience the meaning of the terms: "Dictatorship of the Proletariat," and "Soviet Power"; and 2) to point out in what could and should consist in all countries the immediate and systematic preparatory work to realize these formulae; and 3) to indicate the ways and means of curing our movement of its defects.

1. The Substance of the Dictatorship of the Proletariat and of the Soviet Power

2. The victory of Socialism (as the first stage of Communism) over capitalism demands the accomplishment of

the three following tasks by the proletariat, as the only really revolutionary class:

The first is to lay low the exploiters, and first of all the bourgeoisie as their chief economic and political representative; to completely defeat them; to crush their resistance; to render impossible any attempts on their part to reinstate the yoke of capitalism and wage-slavery.

The second is to inspire and lead in the footsteps of the revolutionary advance guard of the proletariat, its Communist party—not only the whole proletariat or its large majority, but the entire mass of workers and those exploited by capital, to enlighten, organize, instruct, and discipline them during the course of the bold and mercilessly firm struggle against the exploiters; to wrench this enormous majority of the population in all the capitalist countries out of their state of dependence on the bourgeoisie; to instil in them through practical experience confidence in the leading role of the proletariat and its revolutionary advance guard. The third is to neutralize or render harmless the inevitable fluctuations between the bourgeoisie and the proletariat, between bourgeois democracy and Soviet Power, on the part of that rather numerous class in all advanced countries— although constituting a minority of the population—the small owners and proprietors in agriculture, industry, commerce, and the corresponding layers of intellectuals, employees and so on.

The first and second tasks are independent ones, demanding each of them its special methods of action in respect to the exploiters and to the exploited. The third task results from the two first, demanding only a skilful, timely, flexible combination of the methods of the first and second kind, depending on the concrete circumstances of each separate case of fluctuation.

3. Under the circumstances which have been created in the whole world, and most of all in the most advanced, powerful, most enlightened and free capitalist countries by militarism, imperialism, oppression of colonies and the weaker nations, the universal imperialist slaughter the "peace" of Versailles, to admit the idea of a voluntary submission of the capitalists to the will of the majority of the exploited—of a peaceful, reformist passage to Socialism—is not only to give proof of an extreme petty bourgeois obtuseness, but it is a direct deceiving of the workmen, a disguising of capitalist wage-slavery, a concealment of truth. This truth consists in the fact that the bourgeoisie, the most enlightened and democratic bourgeoisie, is even now not stopping before deceit and crime, before the slaughter of millions of workmen and peasants, for the retainment of the right of private ownership over the means of production. Only a violent defeat of the bourgeoisie, the confiscation of its property, the annihilation of the entire bourgeois government apparatus, from top to bottom, parliamentary, juridical, military, bureaucratic, administrative, municipal, etc., up to the individual exile or internment of the most stubborn and dangerous exploiters, the establishment of a strict control over them for the repressing of all inevitable attempts at resistance and restoration of capitalist slavery—only such measures will be able to guarantee the complete submission of the whole class of exploiters.

On the other hand it is the same disguising of capitalism and bourgeois democracy, the same deceiving of the workmen, when the old parties and old leaders of the Second International admit the idea that the majority of the workers and exploited will be able to acquire a clear Socialist consciousness, firm Socialist convictions and character under the conditions of capitalist enslavement, under the yoke of

44

the bourgeoisie, which assumes an endless variety of forms—
the more refined and at the same time the more cruel and
pitiless, the more cultured is the given capitalist nation. In
reality it is only when the advance guard of the proletariat,
supported by the whole class as the only revolutionary one,
or a majority of the same, will have overthrown the exploiters, crushed them, freed all the exploited from their
position of slaves, improved their conditions of life immediately at the expense of the expropriated capitalists—only
after that, and during the very course of the acute class
struggle, will it be possible to realize the enlightenment,
education and organization of the widest masses of workers
and exploited around the proletariat, under its influence and
direction, to cure them of their egotism, their non-solidarity,
their vices and weaknesses engendered by private ownership,
and to transform them into a free union of free workers.

4. For the success of the victory over capitalism, a correct
correlation between the leading Communist Party,—if it is
really the advanced guard of the revolutionary class, if it
includes the best representatives of the class, if it consists
of perfectly conscious and loyal Communists, enlightened
by the experience gained in the stubborn revolutionary struggle—only if this party is able to become bound indissolubly
with the entire life of its class, and through the latter with
the whole mass of the exploited, and to inspire full confidence in this class and this mass, only such a party is capable
of leading the proletariat in the most pitiless, decisive, last
struggle against all the forces of capitalism. On the other
hand, only under the leadership of such a party will the
proletariat be able to employ all the force of its revolutionary onslaught, nullifying the inevitable apathy and partial
resistance of the insignificant minority of the demoralized
labor aristocracy, the old trade-union and guild leaders, etc.

45

Only then will the proletariat be able to display its power which is immeasurably greater than its share in the population, by reason of the economic organization of capitalist society itself. Lastly, only when practically freed from the yoke of the bourgeoisie and the bourgeois government apparatus, only after acquiring the possibility of freely (from all capitalist exploitation) organizing into its own Soviets, will the mass—i.e., the total of all the workers and exploited—develop for the first time in history all the initiative and energy of tens of millions of people, formerly crushed by capitalism. Only when the Soviets will become the only State apparatus will effectual participation in the administration be realized for the entire mass of the exploited, who even under the most cultured and free bourgeois democracy remained practically excluded from participation in the administration. Only in the Soviets does the mass really begin to study, not out of books, but out of its own practical experience, the work of Socialist construction, the creation of a new social discipline, a free union of free workers.

2. In What Should the Immediate and Universal Preparation for Dictatorship of the Proletariat Consist?

5. The present moment in the development of the International Communist movement is characterized by the fact that in a great majority of capitalist countries the preparation of the proletariat to the realization of its dictatorship is not yet completed—very often it has not even been begun systematically. It does not follow that the proletarian revolution is not possible in the most immediate

future; it is quite possible, because the economic and political situation is extraordinarily rich in inflammable material and causes of its sudden inflammation; the other condition for a revolution, besides the preparedness of the proletariat, namely, the general state of crisis in all the ruling and bourgeois parties, is also at hand. But it follows from the above that the duty for the moment of the Communist parties consists not in accelerating the revolution, but in extensively preparing the proletariat for it. On the other hand, the above instance in the history of many Socialist parties draws our attention to the fact, that the "recognition" of the dictatorship of the proletariat should not remain only verbal.

Therefore the principal duty of the Communist parties, from the point of view of an international proletarian movement, is at the present moment the uniting of the dispersed Communist forces, the formation in each country of a single Communist party (or the strengthening and renovation of the already existing one) in order to multiply the work of preparing the proletariat for the conquest of the governing power, and especially for the acquisition of the power in the form of a dictatorship of the proletariat. The ordinary Socialist work of groups and parties recognizing the proletarian dictatorship has not been sufficiently subjected to the radical transformation, the radical renovation which is necessary for it to be recognized as Communist work, and corresponding to the tasks on the eve of proletarian dictatorship.

6. The conquest of political power by the proletariat does not put a stop to its class struggle against the bourgeoisie; on the contrary it makes the struggle especially broad, acute and pitiless. All the groups, parties, leaders of the labor movement, fully or partially on the side of reformism, the

"center" and so on, turn inevitably, during the most acute moments of the struggle, either to the side of the bourgeoisie or to that of the fluctuating ones, or the most dangerous add to the number of the unreliable friends of the victorious proletariat. Therefore the preparation for the dictatorship of the proletariat demands not only an increased struggle against all reformist and "centrist" tendencies, but a modification of the nature of this struggle.

The struggle should not be limited to an explanation of the erroneousness of such tendencies, but any leader in the labor movement who may be manifesting such tendencies should be persistently and mercilessly denounced, otherwise the proletariat will not know whom it must trust in the most decisive struggle against the bourgeoisie. This struggle is such, that at any moment it may replace and has replaced, as experience has proved, the weapon of criticism by the criticism of the weapon. The least vacillation or weakness in the denunciation of those who show themselves to be reformists or "centrists," means a direct increase of the danger of the power of the proletariat being overthrown by the bourgeoisie, which will on the morrow utilize in favor of the counter-revolution all that which to short-sighted people appears only as a "theoretical difference of opinion" to-day.

7. In particular one cannot stop at the usual doctrinaire refutation of all "collaboration" between the proletariat and the bourgeoisie.

The simple defense of "liberty and equality," under the condition of preserving the right of private ownership of the means of production, becomes transformed under the conditions of the dictatorship of the proletariat—which will never be able at once to destroy completely all private ownership—into a "collaboration" with the bourgeoisie, which undermines directly the power of the working class. The dictatorship of the proletariat means the strengthening and defense, by means of the ruling power of the State, of the "non-liberty" of the exploiter to continue his work of oppression and exploitation, the "inequality" of the proprietor (i.e., of the person who has taken for himself personally the means of production socially created), in comparison with the propertiless class. That which before the victory of the proletariat seems but a theoretical difference of opinion on the question of "democracy," becomes inevitably on the morrow, after the victory, a question which can only be decided by force of arms. Consequently, without a radical modification of the whole nature of the struggle against the "centrists" and "defenders of democracy," even a preliminary preparation of the masses for the realization of dictatorship of the proletariat is impossible.

8. The dictatorship of the proletariat is the most decisive and revolutionary form of class struggle between the proletariat and the bourgeoisie. Such a struggle can be successful only when the most revolutionary advance guard of the proletariat leads the greatest majority of it. The preparation of the dictatorship of the proletariat demands therefore not only the elucidation of the bourgeois nature of all reformism, all defense of "democracy," with the preservation of the right to the private ownership of the means of production; not only the denunciation of such tendencies, which in practice mean the defense of the bourgeoisie inside the labor movement—but it demands also the replacing of the old leaders by Communists in all kinds of proletarian organizations, not only political, but economic, co-operative, educational, etc. The more lasting, complete and solid the rule of the bourgeois democracy has been in any country, the more has it been possible for the bourgeoisie to appoint as labor leaders men who have been educated by it, imbued with its

views and prejudices and very frequently directly or indirectly bribed by it. It is necessary to act more aggressively than in the past to remove all these representatives of the labor aristocracy, or such bourgeois minded workmen, from their posts and replace them by even inexperienced workers, so long as these are in close contact with the exploited masses, and enjoy the latter's confidence in the struggle against the exploiters. The dictatorship of the proletariat will demand the appointment of such inexperienced workmen to the most responsible State functions, otherwise the rule of the labor government will be powerless and it will not have the support of the masses.

9. The dictatorship of the proletariat is the most complete realization of a leadership over all workers and exploited, who have been oppressed, beaten down, crushed, intimidated, dispersed, deceived by the class of capitalists, on the part of the only class prepared for such a leading role by the whole history of capitalism. Therefore the preparation of the dictatorship of the proletariat must be begun immediately and in all places by means of the following method, among others:

In every organization, union, association—beginning with the proletarian ones at first, and afterwards in all those of the non-proletarian workers and exploited masses (political, professional, military, co-operative, educational, sporting, etc., etc.), must be formed groups or nuclei of Communists —mostly open ones, but also secret ones which become necessary in each case when the arrest or exile of their members or the dispersal of the organization is threatened; and these nuclei, in close contact with one another and with the central party, exchanging experiences, carrying on the work of propaganda, campaign, organization, adapting themselves to all the branches of social life, to all the various forms and subdivisions of the working masses, must systematically train themselves, the party, the class and the masses by such multiform work.

At the same time it is most important to work out practically the different methods on the one hand in respect to the "leaders" or responsible representatives, who are very frequently hopelessly infected with petty bourgeois and imperialist prejudices; these "leaders" must be mercilessly denounced and driven out of the labor movement. On the other hand, in respect to the masses, who, especially after the imperialist slaughter, are mostly inclined to listen to and accept the doctrine of the necessity of leadership of the proletariat as the only way out of capitalistic enslavement, the masses must be approached with patience and caution, and with an understanding of the peculiarities, and the special psychology of each stratum.

10. In particular one of the groups or nuclei of the Communists deserves the special attention and care of the party, namely, the parliamentary faction, i.e., the group of members of the party who are members of bourgeois representative institutions (first of all state institutions, then local, municipal and others). On the one hand, such a tribune has a special importance in the eyes of the wider circles of the backward working masses imbued with petit bourgeois prejudices, therefore from this very tribune the Communists must carry on their work of propaganda, agitation, organization, explaining to the masses why the dispersal of bourgeois parliament (Constituent Assembly) by the national Congress of Soviets was a legitimate proceeding at the time in Russia (as it will be in all countries in due time). On the other hand, the whole history of the bourgeois democracy has made out of the parliamentary tribune, especially in the more advanced countries, the chief or one of the chief

51

means of unbelievable financial and political swindles, the possibility of making a career, hypocrisy, oppression of the workers. Therefore the deep hatred against all parliaments on the part of the best representatives of the revolutionary proletariat is perfectly justified. Therefore on the part of the Communist parties, and all parties joining the Third International, especially in cases when such parties have been formed not by means of a split in the old parties and after a lasting stubborn struggle against them, but by means of the whole party accepting (often nominally) a new position, it is necessary to be very strict in their attitude towards their parliamentary factions, demanding their complete subordination to the control and the directions of the Central Committee of the party; to include in them mostly revolutionary workmen; to subject their parliamentary speeches to a most careful analysis in the party meetings and in the party press, from the point of view of their Communist integrity; to detail the parliament members for propaganda among the masses; to exclude from such factions all those who show a tendency towards the Second International, and so forth.

11. One of the chief causes of retarding the revolutionary labor movement in the advanced capitalist countries lies in the fact that owing to colonial dominions and super-dividends of financial capital, etc., capital has been able to separate a comparatively more solid and broader group of a small minority of the labor aristocracy. The latter enjoys better conditions and wages and is most of all impregnated with the spirit of craft narrowmindedness, petit bourgeois and imperialist prejudices. This is the true social "support" of the Second International reformists and centrists, and at the present moment almost the chief social support of the bourgeoisie.

Not even preliminary preparation of the proletariat for

the overthrow of the bourgeoisie is possible without an immediate, systematic, widely organized and open struggle against this group which undoubtedly—as experience has already proved—will furnish plenty of men for the White Guards of the bourgeoisie, after the victory of the proletariat. All the parties joining to the Third International must at all costs put into practice the slogan; "in closer contact with the masses," understanding by the word "masses" the entire mass of workers and those exploited by capitalism, especially the less organized and enlightened, the most oppressed and less adaptable to organization.

The proletariat becomes revolutionary only in so far as it is not enclosed within narrow guild limits, in so far as it participates in all the activities of public life, as a leader of the whole working and exploited mass; and it is completely impossible for it to realize its dictatorship unless it is ready for and capable of sacrificing everything for the victory over the bourgeoisie. The experience of Russia in this respect has a theoretical and practical importance; where the proletariat could not have realized its dictatorship, nor acquired the respect and confidence of the whole working mass, if it had not borne most of the sacrifices and had not suffered from hunger more than all the other strata of this mass during the most difficult moments of the onslaught, war and blockade on the part of the world bourgeoisie.

In particular it is necessary for the Communist Party and the whole advanced proletariat to give the most absolute support to every spontaneous mass strike movement, which is alone able under the yoke of capitalism to awaken, properly arouse, enlighten, and organize the masses, and develop in them a full confidence in the leading role of the revolutionary proletariat. Without such a preparation no dictatorship of the proletariat will be possible, and those who are

53

capable of preaching against strikes, like Kautsky in Germany, Turatti in Italy, are not to be suffered in the ranks of parties joining the Third International. This concerns still more, naturally, such trade-union and parliamentary leaders, who often betray the workman by teaching them to make the strike an instrument of reformism and not of revolution (Jouhaux in France, Gompers in America, and Thomas in England).

12. For all countries, even for most free "legal" and "peaceful" ones in the sense of a lesser acuteness in the class struggle the period has arrived, when it has become absolutely necessary for every Communist party to combine systematically all legal and illegal work, legal and illegal organization.

In the most enlightened and free countries, with a most "solid" bourgeois-democratic regime, the governments are systematically resorting, in spite of their false and hypocritical assurances, to the method of keeping secret lists of Communists, to endless violations of their constitutions for the semi-secret support of White Guards and the murder of Communists in all countries, to secret preparations for the arrest of Communists, the introduction of provocators among the Communists, etc. Only the most reactionary petty bourgeoisie, by whatever high-sounding "democratic" or pacifist phrases it might disguise its ideas, can dispute this fact or the necessary conclusion; an immediate formation by all legal Communist parties of illegal organizations for systematic illegal work, for their complete preparation at any moment to thwart persecution on the part of the bourgeoisie. It is especially necessary to carry on illegal work in the army, navy and police, as after the imperialist slaughter all the governments in the world are becoming afraid of the national armies, open to all peasants and workmen, and they

54

are setting up in secret all kinds of select military organizations recruited from the bourgeoisie and specially provided with improved technical military equipment.

On the other hand, it is also necessary in all cases without exception not to limit oneself to illegal work, but to carry on also legal work overcoming all difficulties, founding a legal press and legal organizations under the most diverse circumstances, and in case of need, frequently changing names. This is now being done by the illegal Communist parties in Finland, Hungary, partly in Germany, Poland, Latvia, etc. It is thus that the I. W. W. in America should act, as well as all the legal Communist parties at present, in case prosecutors start prosecutions on the basis of resolutions of the congresses of the Communist International, etc.

The absolute necessity of the principle of combining illegal and legal work is determined not only by the total aggregate of all the peculiarities of the given moment, on the very eve of a proletarian dictatorship, but by the necessity of proving to the bourgeoisie, that there is not and can not be any branch of the work of which the Communists could not gain control, and still more by the fact that everywhere there are still wide circles of the proletariat and greater ones of the non-proletarian workers and exploited masses, which still trust in the bourgeois democracy. Our most important duty is to point out to them the fallacy of this conviction.

13. In particular, the situation of the labor press in the more advanced capitalist countries shows with special evidence both the falseness of liberty and equality under bourgeois democracy, and the necessity of a systematic blending of the legal and illegal work. Both in vanquished Germany and in victorious America all the power of the governmental apparatus of the bourgeoisie, and all the tricks of its financial

kings are being set in motion in order to deprive the workmen of their press; prosecutions and arrest (or murder by
means of hired murderers) of the editors, prohibition of
sending by mail, depriving of paper, etc. Moreover, the
information necessary for a daily paper is in the hands of
bourgeois telegraph agencies, and the advertisements, without which a large paper cannot pay its way, are at the "free"
disposal of capitalists. On the whole, by means of deceit,
the pressure of capital and the bourgeois government, the
bourgeoisie deprives the revolutionary proletariat of its press.

For the struggle against this state of things, the Communist parties must create a new type of periodical press
for extensive circulation among the workmen: 1) Legal
publications, in which the Communists without calling
themselves such and without mentioning their connection
with the party, would learn to utilize the slightest possibility
allowed by the laws as the Bolsheviki did at the time of the
Tzar, after 1905.

2) Illegal sheets, although of the smallest dimensions and
irregularly published, but reproduced in most of the printing offices by workmen (in secret, or if the movement has
grown stronger, by means of a revolutionary seizure of the
printing offices), and giving the proletariat undiluted revolutionary information and the revolutionary slogans.

Without involving the masses in the revolutionary struggle for a free Communist press the preparation for the dictatorship of the proletariat is impossible.

3. The Changing of the Policy
and Partly Also of the Make-up of the Parties
Joining or Willing to Join The Communist International

14. The degree of preparedness of the proletariat to carry out its dictatorship, in the countries most important from the viewpoint of world economics and world politics, is manifested most objectively and precisely by the fact that the most influential parties of the Second International, the French Socialist Party, the Independent Social Democratic Party of Germany, the Independent Labour Party of England, the American Socialist Party, have gone out of this yellow International and have passed resolutions to join the Third International conditionally. This proves that not only the advance guard but the majority of the revolutionary proletariat has begun to pass over to our side, persuaded thereto by the whole course of events. The chief thing now is to know how to complete this transition of the revolutionary proletariat to our side in order to solidify and strengthen that which has been attained so as to be able to advance along the whole line, without the slightest hesitation.

15. The whole activity of the above-mentioned parties (to which must be added the Swiss Socialist Party, if the telegraphic reports regarding its resolution to join the Third International are correct) proves—and any given periodical paper of these parties confirms it—that they are not Communist as yet, and frequently even are in direct opposition to the fundamental principles of the Third International, namely: the recognition of the dictatorship of the proletariat, and of Soviet power instead of the bourgeois democracy.

57

Therefore the Second Congress of the Communist International announces that it does not consider it possible to receive these parties immediately; that it confirms the answer of the Executive Committee of the Third International to the German Independents; that it confirms its readiness to carry on negotiations with any party leaving the Second International and desiring to join the Third; that it grants the right of a consultative vote to the delegate of such parties at all its congresses and conferences, and that it proposes the following conditions for a complete union of these (and similar) parties with the Communist International:

1. The publishing of all the resolutions passed by all the congresses of the Communist International and by the Executive Committee, in all the periodical publications of the party.

2. Their discussion at the special meetings of all sections and local organizations of the party.

3. The convocation of a special congress of the party for the purpose of summarizing the conclusion of the discussion and for

4. Expulsion from the party of all elements who persist in their adherence to the Second International.

5. The transfer of all periodical papers of the party into the hands of Communist editors.

6. The parties which are now desirous of joining the Third International but have not yet radically modified their former tactics, must previously see to it that their central committee and their most important central institutions should consist by two-thirds of such comrades who have openly declared themselves to be partisans of the adhesion of the party to the Third International before the Second Congress. Exceptions to this rule may be allowed with the

58

approval of the Executive Committee of the Communist International. Likewise the Executive Committee is entitled to make exceptions in regard to representatives of centrist tendencies, as mentioned in paragraph 7.

7. Members of the party who repudiate the conditions and theses adopted by the Communist International must be excluded from the Party. The same applies to delegates of special congresses.

The Second Congress of the Third International must charge its Executive Committee to admit the above-named and similar parties into the Third International after a preliminary verification that all these conditions have been fulfilled, and that the nature of the activity of the party has become Communist.

16. In regard to the question as to what must be the line of conduct of the Communists at present constituting the minority at the responsible posts of the above-named and similar parties, the Second Congress of the Third International should establish, that in view of the evident growth of the sincerest sympathies for Communism among the workmen belonging to these parties, it would be undesirable for the Communists to leave the parties, so long as they are able to carry on their work within the parties in the spirit of a recognition of the dictatorship of the proletariat and Soviet power and so long as criticism of all opportunists and centrists remaining in these parties is possible.

However, as soon as the left wing of the centrist party becomes sufficiently strong it can leave the party in a body and form a Communist Party, should this appear useful for the development of Communism.

At the same time the Second Congress of the Third International must declare itself in favor of the Communist Party, and the groups and organizations sympathizing with

Communism in England, joining the Labour Party, notwithstanding the circumstance that this party is a member of the Second International. The reason for this is that so long as this party will allow all constituent organizations their present freedom of criticism and freedom of propaganda, and organizational activity in favor of the dictatorship of the proletariat and the power of Soviets, so long as this party preserves its principle of uniting all the economic organizations of the working class, the Communists ought to take all measures and even consent to certain compromises, in order to be able to exercise an influence over the wider circles of workmen and the masses, to denounce their opportunist leaders from a higher tribune, to accelerate the transfer of the political power from the direct representatives of the bourgeoisie to the "labor lieutenants of the capitalist class," so that the masses may be more rapidly cured of all illusions on this subject.

17. With regard to the Italian Socialist Party the Second Congress of the Third International recognizes that the revision of the program, which had been last year decided upon by the Party Congress of Bologne, indicates a milestone along the road of Communism and that the proposal which was submitted to the National Council of the Italian Socialist Party by the Turin section of the party published in the journal "L'Ordine Nuovo" ("The New Order") of the 3rd of May, 1920, is in keeping with all the basic principles of the Third International. The Third International requests that at the next congress of the Italian Socialist Party, which is to be convened in accordance with the party regulations and the general rules regarding the affiliation to the Third International, the Italian Socialist Party should discuss these proposals as well as all the decisions of the two congresses of the Communist International, especial

attention to be paid to the resolutions on parliamentary fractions, trade unions and non-Communist elements of the party.

18. The Second Congress of the Third International considers as not correct the views regarding the relations of the party to the class and to the masses, and the non-participation of the Communist parties in the bourgeois parliaments and reactionary labor unions, which have been emphatically repudiated in the special resolutions of the present congress, and defended in full by the "Communist Labor Party of Germany" and also partially by the "Communist Party of Switzerland," by the organ of the West European secretariat of the Communist International "Communismus" in Vienna, and by several of our Dutch comrades; further by certain Communist organizations in England, as for instances "The Workers' Socialist Federation," also by the "I. W. W." in America, the "Shop Steward Committees" in England, and so forth.

Nevertheless the Second Congress of the Third International considers possible and desirable the immediate affiliation of such of these organizations which have not already done so officially, because in the given case, especially as regards the I. W. W. of America and Australia, and the "Shop Steward Committees" of England, we have to deal with a genuinely proletarian mass movement, which practically adheres to the principles of the Communist International. In such organizations any mistaken views on the question of participation in the bourgeois parliaments are to be explained not so much by the role of members of the bourgeoisie advocating their own petty bourgeois views as the views of the Anarchists frequently are, but by the political inexperience of proletarians who are, nevertheless, completely revolutionary and in contact with the masses.

61

The Second Congress of the Third International requests therefore all the Communist organizations and groups in the Anglo-Saxon countries, even in case immediate union between the Third International and the "Industrial Workers of the World" and the "Shop Steward Committees" does not take place, to carry on a policy of the most friendly attitude toward these organizations, to enter into closer connection with them, to explain to them and the masses sympathizing with them in a friendly way, from the point of view of all revolutions and the three Russian revolutions in the Twentieth Century especially, the erroneousness of their above-stated views, and not to desist from repeated attempts to become united with these organizations so as to form one Communist Party.

19. In connection with this the Congress draws the attention of all comrades, especially in the Latin and Anglo-Saxon countries, to the fact that among the Anarchists since the war all over the world a deep ideological scission is taking place upon the question of their attitude towards the dictatorship of the proletariat and the power of Soviets. And it is just among the proletarian elements, which were frequently led into anarchism by their perfectly justified hatred of the opportunism and reformism of the parties of the Second International, that there is to be noticed a perfectly correct understanding of these principles, especially among those who are more nearly acquainted with the experience of Russia, Finland, Hungary, Lettland, Poland, and Germany.

The congress considers it the duty of all comrades to support by all measures all the masses of proletarian elements passing from anarchism to the Third International. The congress points out that the success of the work of the truly Communist parties ought to be measured, among other things, by how far they have been able to attract to their party all the bona fide proletarian masses from anarchism.

CONDITIONS OF ADMISSION
TO THE COMMUNIST INTERNATIONAL

THE FIRST CONSTITUENT CONGRESS of the Communist International did not draw up precise conditions of admission to the Third International.

At the moment of the convocation of the First Congress in the majority of countries only Communist currents and groups existed.

The Second World Congress of the Communist International is convening under different conditions. At the present moment in most countries there are not only Communist tendencies and groups but Communist parties and organizations.

The Communist International more and more frequently receives applications from parties and groups but a short time ago belonging to the Second International, now desirous of joining the Third International, but not yet really Communists. The Second International is completely broken. Seeing the complete helplessness of the Second International, the intermediary faction and the groups of the "centre" are trying to lean on the ever strengthening Communist International, hoping at the same time, however, to preserve a certain "autonomy" which should enable them to carry on their former opportunist or "centrist" policy. The Communist International has become the fashion.

The desire of certain leading groups of the "centre" to join the Third International now is an indirect confirmation of the fact that the Communist International has gained the sympathy of the majority of conscious workers of the

64

whole world and that it is growing stronger every day.

The Communist International is being threatened with the danger of dilution with the fluctuating and half-and-half groups which have as yet not abandoned the ideology of the Second International.

It must be mentioned that in some of the large parties (Italy, Norway, Jugo-Slavia, etc.), the majority of which adhere to the point of view of Communism, there is up to this moment a considerable reformist and social pacifist wing, which is only awaiting the moment to revive and to begin an active "sabotage" of the proletarian revolution, and thus assist the bourgeoisie and the Second International.

No Communist should forget the lesson of the Hungarian Soviet Republic.

The unity between the Hungarian Communists and the so-called Left Social Democrats cost the Hungarian proletariat very dear.

In view of this the Second World Congress finds it necessary to establish most definite conditions for the joining of new parties, as well as to point out to such parties as have already joined the Communist International the duties which are laid upon them.

The Second Congress of the Communist International rules that the conditions for joining the Communist International shall be as follows:

1. The general propaganda and agitation should bear a really Communist character, and should correspond to the program and decisions of the Third International. The entire party press should be edited by reliable Communists who have proved their loyalty to the cause of the proletarian revolution. The dictatorship of the proletariat should not be spoken of simply as a current hackneyed formula, it should be advocated in such a way that its necessity should

be apparent to every rank-and-file workingman and working-woman, to each soldier and peasant, and should emanate from every-day facts, systematically recorded by our press day by day.

All periodical and other publications, as well as all party publications and editions, are subject to the control of the presidium of the party, independently of whether the party is legal or illegal. It should in no way be permitted that the publishers abuse their autonomy and carry on a policy not fully corresponding to the policy of the party.

Wherever the followers of the Third International have access, and whatever means of propaganda are at their disposal, whether the columns of newspapers, popular meetings, labor unions or co-operatives,—it is indispensable for them not only to denounce the bourgeoisie, but also its assistants and agents—reformists of every color and shade.

2. Every organization desiring to join the Communist International shall be bound systematically and regularly to remove from all the responsible posts in the labor movement (party organization, editorship, labor unions, parliamentary factions, co-operatives, municipalities, etc.) all reformists and followers of the "centre," and to have them replaced by Communists, even at the cost of replacing at the beginning "experienced" opportunists by rank-and-file workingmen.

3. The class struggle in almost every country of Europe and America is entering the phase of civil war. Under such conditions the Communists can have no confidence in bourgeois laws. They should create everywhere a parallel illegal apparatus, which at the decisive moment should be of assistance to the party to do its duty toward the revolution. In every country where, in consequence of martial law or of other exceptional laws, the Communists are unable to

carry on their work legally, a combination of legal and illegal work is absolutely necessary.

4. Persistent and systematic propaganda and agitation must be carried on in the army, where Communist groups should be formed in every military organization. Wherever owing to repressive legislation agitation becomes impossible, it is necessary to carry on such agitation illegally. But refusal to carry on or participate in such work should be considered equal to treason to the revolutionary cause, and incompatible with affiliation to the Third International.

5. A systematic and regular propaganda is necessary in the rural districts. The working class can gain no victory unless it possesses the sympathy and support of at least part of the rural workers and of the poor peasants, and unless other sections of the population are equally utilized. Communist work in the rural districts is acquiring a predominant importance during the present period. It should be carried on through Communist workmen of both city and country who have connections with the rural districts. To refuse to do this work, or to transfer such work to untrustworthy half reformists, is equal to renouncing the proletarian revolution.

6. Every party desirous of affiliating to the Third International should renounce not only avowed social patriotism, but also the falsehood and the hypocrisy of social pacifism: It should systematically demonstrate to the workers that without a revolutionary overthrow of capitalism no international arbitration, no talk of disarmament, no democratic reorganization of the League of Nations will be capable of saving mankind from new imperialist wars.

7. Parties desirous of joining the Communist International must recognize the necessity of a complete and absolute rupture with reformism and the policy of the "centrists," and must advocate this rupture amongst the widest

circles of the party membership, without which condition a consistent Communist policy is impossible. The Communist International demands unconditionally and peremptorily that such rupture be brought about with the least possible delay. The Communist International cannot reconcile itself to the fact that such avowed reformists as for instance Turatti, Modigliani, Kautsky, Hilferding, Hillquit, Longuet, Macdonald and others should be entitled to consider themselves members of the Third International. This would make the Third International resemble the Second International.

8. In the Colonial question and that of the oppressed nationalities, there is necessary an especially distinct and clear line of conduct of the parties of countries where the bourgeoisie possesses such colonies or oppresses other nationalities. Every party desirous of belonging to the Third International should be bound to denounce without any reserve all the methods of "its own" imperialists in the colonies, supporting not in words only but practically a movement of liberation in the colonies. It should demand the expulsion of its own imperialists from such colonies, and cultivate among the workmen of its own country a truly fraternal attitude towards the working population of the colonies and oppressed nationalities, and carry on a systematic agitation in its own army against every kind of oppression of the colonial population.

9. Every party desirous of belonging to the Communist International should be bound to carry on systematic and persistent Communist work in the labor unions, co-operatives and other organizations of working masses. It is necessary to form Communist nuclei within these organizations, which by persistent and lasting work should win over labor unions to Communism. These nuclei should constantly

denounce the treachery of the social patriots and of the fluctuations of the "centre." These Communist nuclei should be completely subordinated to the party in general.

10. Any party belonging to the Communist International is bound to carry on a stubborn struggle against the Amsterdam "International" of the yellow labor unions. It should propagate insistently amongst the organized workers the necessity of a rupture with the yellow Amsterdam International. It should support by all means in its power the International Unification of Red Labor Unions joining to the Communist International.

11. Parties desirous of joining the Third International shall be bound to inspect the personnel of their parliamentary factions, to remove all unreliable elements therefrom, to control such factions, not only verbally but in reality, to subordinate them to the Central Committee of the party, and to demand from each Communist representative in parliament to subject his entire activity to the interests of real revolutionary propaganda, and agitation.

12. All the parties belonging to the Communist International should be formed on the basis of the principle of democratic centralization. At the present time of acute civil war the Communist Party will only be able fully to do its duty when it is organized in a sufficiently centralized manner; when it possesses an iron discipline and when its party centre enjoys the confidence of the party membership and is endowed with complete power, authority and ample rights.

13. The Communist parties of those countries where the Communist activity is legal should clean out their members from time to time, as well as those of the party organizations, in order to systematically free the party from the petty bourgeois elements which penetrate into it.

69

14. Each party desirous of affiliating to the Communist International should be obliged to render every possible assistance to the Soviet Republics in their struggle against all counter-revolutionary forces. The Communist parties should carry on a precise and definite propaganda to induce the workers to refuse to transport any kind of military equipment intended for fighting against the Soviet Republics, and should also by legal or illegal means carry on a propaganda amongst the troops sent against the workers' republics, etc.

15. All those parties which up to the present moment have stood upon the old social democratic programs should within the shortest time possible draw up a new Communist program in conformity with the special conditions of their country, and in accordance with the resolutions of the Communist International. As a rule the program of each party belonging to the Communist International should be confirmed by the next congress of the Communist International or its Executive Committee. In the event of the failure of the program of any party being confirmed by the Executive Committee of the Communist International, the said party shall be entitled to appeal to the congress of the Communist International.

16. All the resolutions of the congresses of the Communist International, as well as the resolutions of the Executive Committee are binding for all parties joining the Communist International. The Communist International, operating under the conditions of most acute civil warfare, should be centralized in a better manner than the Second International. At the same time, the Communist International and the Executive Committee are naturally bound in every form of their activity to consider the variety of conditions under which the different parties have to work and struggle,

and generally binding resolutions should be passed only on such questions upon which such resolutions are possible.

17. In connection with the above, all parties desiring to join the Communist International should alter their names. Each party desirous of joining the Communist International should bear the following name: Communist Party of such and such a country, section of the Third Communist International. The question of the party name is not only a formal one, but is a political question of great importance. The Communist International has declared a decisive war against the entire bourgeois world, and all the yellow Social Democratic parties. It is indispensable that every rank-and-file worker should be able clearly to distinguish between the Communist parties and the old official "Social-Democratic" or "Socialist" parties, which have betrayed the cause of the working class.

18. All the leading organs of the press of every party are bound to publish all the most important documents of the Executive Committee of the Communist International.

19. All parties which have joined the Communist International as well as those which have expressed a desire to do so are obliged in as short a space of time as possible, and in no case later than four months after the Second Congress of the Communist International, to convene an Extraordinary Congress in order to discuss these conditions. In addition to this, the Central Committees of these parties should take care to acquaint all its local organizations with the regulations of the Second Congress.

20. All those parties which at the present time are willing to join the Third International, but have so far not changed their tactics in any radical manner, should, prior to their joining the Third International, take care that not less than two-thirds of their committee members and of all their cen-

tral institutions should be composed of comrades who have made an open and definite declaration prior to the convening of the Second Congress, as to their desire that the party should affiliate to the Third International. Exceptions are permitted only with the consent of the Executive Committee of the Third International. The Executive Committee of the Communist International has the right to make an exception also for the representatives of the "centre" as mentioned in paragraph 7.

21. Those members of the party who reject in principle the conditions and the theses of the Third International, are liable to be excluded from the party.

This applies also to the delegates at the special congresses of the party.

ROLE OF THE COMMUNIST PARTY
IN THE PROLETARIAN REVOLUTION

THE WORLD PROLETARIAT is confronted with decisive battles. We are living in an epoch of civil war. The critical hour has struck. In almost all countries where there is a labor movement of any importance the working class, arms in hand, stands in the midst of fierce and decisive battles. Now more than ever is the working class in need of a strong organization. Without losing an hour of invaluable time, the working class must keep on indefatigably preparing for the impending decisive struggle.

The first heroic uprising of the French proletariat during the Paris Commune of 1871 would have been much more successful, and many errors and shortcomings would have been avoided, had there been a strong Communist party, no matter how small. The struggle which the proletariat is now facing, under changed historical circumstances, will be of much more vital importance to the future destiny of the working class than was the insurrection of 1871.

The Second World Congress of the Communist International therefore calls upon the revolutionary workers of the whole world to concentrate all their attention on the following:

1. The Communist Party is part of the working class, namely, its most advanced, class-conscious, and therefore most revolutionary part. The Communist Party is formed of the best, most intelligent, self-sacrificing and far-seeing workers. The Communist Party has no other interests than those of the working class. It differs from the general mass of the workers in that it takes a general view of the whole

historical march of the working class, and at all turns of the road it endeavors to defend the interests, not of separate groups or professions, but of the working class as a whole. The Communist Party is the organized political lever by means of which the more advanced part of the working class leads all the proletarian and semi-proletarian mass, in the right direction.

2. Until the time when the power of government will have been finally conquered by the proletariat, until the time when the proletarian rule will have been firmly established beyond the possibility of a bourgeois restoration, the Communist Party will have in its organized ranks only a minority of the workers. Up to the time when the power will have been seized by it, and during the transition period, the Communist Party may, under favorable conditions, exercise undisputed moral and political influence on all the proletarian and semi-proletarian classes of the population; but it will not be able to unite them within its ranks. Only when the proletarian dictatorship has deprived the bourgeoisie of such powerful weapons as the press, the school, parliament, church, the government apparatus, etc., only when the final overthrow of the capitalist order will have become an evident fact—only then will all or almost all the workers enter the ranks of the Communist Party.

3. A sharp distinction must be made between the conception of "party" and "class." The members of the "Christian" and liberal trade unions of Germany, England and other countries, are undoubtedly parts of the working class. More or less considerable circles of the working people, followers of Scheidemann, Gompers and Co., are likewise part of the working class. Under certain historical conditions the working class is very likely to be impregnated with numerous reactionary elements. The task of Communism is not to

adapt itself to such retrograde elements of the working class, but to raise the whole working class to the level of the Communist vanguard. The confounding of these two conceptions—of party and of class—can only lead to the greatest errors and confusion. Thus, for instance, it is clear that notwithstanding the disposition or prejudices of certain parts of the working masses during the imperialist war, the workers' parties ought to have counteracted these prejudices, defending the historical interests of the proletariat, which demanded of the proletarian parties a declaration of war against war.

Thus in the beginning of the imperialistic war of 1914, the social traitor parties of all countries, in upholding the capitalists of their "own" countries, unanimously declared that such was the will of the people. They forgot at the same time that even if this were so, the duty of the workers' party would have been to combat such an attitude of the majority of the workers, and to defend the interests of the workers at whatever cost. At the very beginning of the Twentieth Century the Russian Mensheviks of that time (the so-called "economists"), denied the possibility of an open political struggle against Tzarism, on the ground that the working class in general was not yet ripe for the understanding of the political struggle. So also has the right wing of the Independents of Germany, in all its compromising, referred to the "will of the masses," failing to understand that the party exists precisely for the purpose of marching ahead of the masses and pointing out the way to them.

4. The Communist International is firmly convinced that the collapse of the old "Social Democratic" parties of the Second International cannot be represented as the collapse of the proletarian party organizations in general. The period of open struggle for the dictatorship of the workers

has created a new proletarian party—the Communist Party.

5. The Communist International emphatically rejects the opinion that the workers could carry out a revolution without having an independent political party of their own. Every class struggle is a political struggle. The object of this struggle, which inevitably turns into a civil war, is the obtaining of political power. However, this power cannot be acquired, organized and directed otherwise than by means of a political party. Only in case the workers have for their leader an organized and experienced party, with strictly defined objects, and a practically drawn-up program of immediate action, both in internal and foreign policy—then only will the acquisition of political power cease to be a casual episode, but it will serve as a starting point for the gradual introduction of the Communist society by the proletariat.

This class struggle likewise demands that the general guidance of the various forms of the proletarian movement (labor unions, factory committees, co-operative associations, cultural-educational work, elections, etc.), be united in one central organization. Only a political party can be such a unifying and guiding centre. To refuse to create and strengthen such a party and submit to its dictates, would mean to abandon the idea of unity in the guidance of the separate proletarian groups, operating on the different arenas of the struggle. Lastly, the class struggle of the proletariat demands a concentrated propaganda, throwing light on the various stages of the fight, a unified point of view, and directing the attention of the proletariat at each given moment to the definite tasks to be accomplished by the whole class. This cannot be done without the help of a centralized political apparatus, i. e., a political party. Therefore the propaganda of the revolutionary Syndicalists, and the partisans of the Industrial Workers of the World (I. W. W.), against the necessity of an independent workers' party, as a matter of fact has only served and continues to serve the interests of the bourgeoisie and the counter-revolutionary "Social-Democrats." In their propaganda against the Communist Party, which the Syndicalists and Industrialists desire to replace by the trade unions or any kind of shapeless, general labor organizations, they approach the opportunists. After the defeat of the revolution in 1905, during the course of several years the Russian Mensheviks proclaimed the necessity of a so-called Labor Congress, which was to replace the revolutionary party of the working class: all kinds of "laborites" of England and America, while consciously carrying on a bourgeois policy, are propagating among the workers the idea of creating indefinite, shapeless workers' unions instead of a political party. The revolutionary Syndicalists and Industrialists desire to fight against the dictatorship of the bourgeoisie, but they do not know how to do it. They do not see that working class without an independent political party is like a body without a head.

Revolutionary Syndicalism and Industrialism are a step forward only in comparison with the old, musty, counter-revolutionary ideology of the Second International. But in comparison with the revolutionary Marxian doctrine, i. e., with Communism, Syndicalism and Industrialism are a step backward. The declaration made by the "lefts" of the Communist Labor Party of Germany (in the program-declaration of their Constituent Congress in April) to the effect that they are forming a party, but not one in the traditional sense of the word ("Kein Partei im ueberlieferten Sinne")—is a capitulation before the views of Syndicalism and Industrialism which are reactionary. The working class cannot achieve the victory over the bourgeoisie by means of the general strike alone, and by the policy of folded arms.

77

The proletariat must resort to an armed uprising. Having understood this, one realizes that an organized political party is absolutely essential, and that shapeless labor organizations will not suffice.

The revolutionary Syndicalists frequently advance the idea of the great importance of a determined revolutionary minority. The Communist Party is just such a determined minority of the working class, which is ready to act, which has a program and strives to organize the masses for the struggle.

6. The most important task of a genuine Communist Party is to preserve constantly the closest contact with the widest masses of the workers. For that purpose the Communists must carry on activity also within such organizations which are non-partisan, but which comprise large proletarian groups, for example, organizations of war invalids in various countries, the "Hands off Russia" Committee in England, Proletarian Tenants' Unions, and so forth. Of special importance are the so-called non-party conferences of workers and peasants held in Russia. Such conferences are being organized almost in every town, in all industrial districts, and in the country. In the elections to these conferences the widest masses even of the most backward workers take part. The order of business at these conferences is made up of the most pressing questions, such as the food question, the housing problem, the military situations, the school question. The Communists exercise their influence on these non-party conferences in the most energetic manner, and with the greatest success for the party. They consider it their most important task to carry on the work of organization and instruction within such organizations. But in order that their efforts should bring forth the desired results, and that such organizations should not become the prey of

opponents of the revolutionary proletariat, the most advanced Communist workers should always have their own independent, closely united Communist Party, working in an organized manner, and standing up for the general interests of Communism at each turn of events, and under every form of the movement.

7. The Communists have no fear of the largest workers' organizations which belong to no party, even when they are of a decidedly reactionary nature (yellow unions, Christian associations, etc.). The Communist Party carries on its work inside such organizations, and untiringly instructs the workers, and proves to them that the idea of no political party as a principle is consciously cultivated among the workers by the bourgeoisie and its labor lieutenants, with the object of keeping the proletariat from an organized struggle for Socialism.

8. The old classical division of the labor movement into three forms (party, labor unions and co-operatives) has evidently served its time. The proletarian revolution in Russia has brought forward the fundamental form of the proletarian dictatorship—the Soviets. The new divisions which are now everywhere forming are: Party, Soviet, Industrial Union. But the party of the proletariat, that is to say, the Communist Party, must constantly and systematically direct the work of the Soviets as well as of the revolutionized industrial unions. The Communist Party, the organized vanguard of the working class, must direct the struggle of the entire class on the economic and the political fields, and also on the field of education. It must be the animating spirit in the industrial unions, workers' councils and all other forms of proletarian organizations.

The origin of the Soviets as an historically basic form of the dictatorship of the proletariat, in no way lessens the

79

guiding role of the Communist Party in the proletarian revolution. The assertions made by the "left" Communists of Germany (in their appeal to the German proletariat of April 14, 1920, signed—"The Communist Labor Party of Germany") that the party must always adapt itself to the idea of the Soviets and assume a proletarian character, is nothing but a hazy expression of the opinion that the Communist Party should dissolve itself into the Soviets, that the Soviets can replace the Communist Party. This idea is essentially mistaken and reactionary.

There was a period in the history of the Russian Revolution when the Soviets were acting in opposition to the party, and supported the policy of the agents of the bourgeoisie. The same has happened in Germany, and may take place in other countries.

In order that the Soviets may be able to perform their historic mission, a strong Communist Party is necessary which should not merely adapt itself to the Soviets, but on the contrary should take care that the Soviets do not adapt themselves to the bourgeoisie, and to the white guard Social Democracy; that with the aid of the Communist factions in the Soviets the latter be brought under the banner of the Communist Party.

Those who propose to the Communist Party to "conform" to the Soviets, those who perceive in such "conformation" a strengthening of the "proletarian nature" of the party, are rendering a bad service both to the party and to the Soviets, and do not understand the importance of the Party, nor that of the Soviets. The stronger the Communist Party in each country, the sooner will the Soviet idea triumph. Many "independent" and even "right" Socialists profess to believe in the Soviet idea. But we cannot prevent such elements from distorting this idea, except if there exists a strong Communist Party, capable of determining the policy of the Soviets and making them follow it.

9. The Communist Party is necessary to the working class not only before it has seized power, not only while it is acquiring such power, but also after the power has passed into the hands of the working class. The history of the Russian Communist Party, for three years at the head of such a vast country, shows that the role of the party after the conquest of power by the working class has not only not diminished, but on the contrary, has greatly increased.

10. On the day of the seizure of power by the proletariat, its party still remained, as formerly, a part of the working class. But it was just that part of the class which organized the victory. During twenty years in Russia—and for a number of years in Germany,—the Communist Party, in its struggle not only against the bourgeoisie, but also against those Socialists who diffuse bourgeois ideas among the proletariat, has enrolled in its ranks the staunchest, most far-seeing and most advanced fighters of the working class. Only by having such a closely united organization of the best part of the working class is it possible for the party to overcome all the difficulties which arise before the proletarian dictatorship in the days following the victory. The organizations of a new proletarian red army, the practical abolition of the bourgeois governing apparatus and the building in its place of the framework of a new proletarian state apparatus, the struggle against the narrow craft tendencies of certain separate groups of workers, the struggle against local and provincial "patriotism," clearing the way for the creation of a new labor discipline—in all these undertakings the final decisive word is to be said by the Communist Party, whose members by their own example animate and guide the majority of the workers.

81

11. The necessity of a political party for the proletariat can cease only with the complete abolition of classes. On the way to this final victory of Communism it is possible that the relative importance of the three fundamental proletarian organizations of modern times (Party, Soviets and Industrial Unions), shall undergo some changes, and that gradually a single type of workers' organization will be formed. The Communist Party, however, will become absorbed in the working class only when Communism ceases to be the object of struggle, and the whole working class shall have become Communist.

12. The Second Congress of the Communist International must not only serve to establish the historical mission of the Communist Party in general, but it must indicate to the international proletariat, in rough draft, what kind of Communist Party is needed.

13. The Communist International assumes that especially during the period of the dictatorship of the proletariat, the Communist Party should be organized on the basis of strict proletarian centralism. In order to lead the working class successfully during the long, stubborn civil war, the Communist Party must establish the strictest military discipline within its own ranks. The experience of the Russian Communist Party in its successful leadership of the civil war of the working class during three years, has proved that the victory of the workers is impossible without a severe discipline, a perfected centralization and the fullest confidence of all the organizations of the party in the leading organ of the party.

14. The Communist Party should be based on the principle of democratic centralization. The chief principle of the latter is the election of the upper party units by those immediately below, the unconditional subordination of

subordinate units to the decisions of those above them, and a strong party central organ, whose decrees are binding upon all the leaders of party life between party conventions.

15. In view of the state of siege introduced by the bourgeoisie against the Communist, a whole series of Communist parties in Europe and America are compelled to exist illegally. It must be remembered that under such conditions it may become necessary sometimes temporarily to deviate from the strict observance of the elective principle, and to delegate to the leading party organizations the right of cooptation, as was done in Russia at one time. Under the state of siege the Communist Party cannot have recourse to a democratic referendum among all the members of the party (as was proposed by part of the American Communists), but on the contrary it should empower its leading central organ to make important decisions in emergencies on behalf of all the members of the party.

16. The doctrine of a wide "autonomy" for the separate local organizations of the party at the present moment only weakens the Communist Party, undermines its working capacity and aids the development of petty bourgeois, anarchistic, centrifugal tendencies.

17. In countries where the power is in the hands of the bourgeoisie or the counter-revolutionary Social Democrats, the Communist Party must learn to unite systematically legal with illegal work; but all legal work must be carried on under the practical control of the illegal party. The parliamentary groups of Communists, both in the central as well as in the local government institutions, must be fully and absolutely subject to the Communist Party in general, irrespective of whether the party on the whole be a legal or an illegal organization at the moment. Any delegate who in one way or another does not submit absolutely to the party shall

83

be expelled from the ranks of Communism.

The legal press (newspapers, publications) must be unconditionally and fully subject to the party in general, and to its central committee. No concessions are admissible in this respect.

18. The fundamental principle of all organization work of the Communist Party and individual Communists must be the creation of Communist nuclei everywhere where they find proletarians and semi-proletarians—although even in small numbers. In every Soviet of Workers' Deputies, in every trade and industrial union, co-operative association, factory, tenants' union, in every government institution, everywhere, even though there may be only three people sympathizing with Communism, a Communist nucleus must be immediately organized. It is only the power of organization of the Communists that enables the advance guard of the working class to be the leader of the whole class. Communist nuclei working in organizations adhering to no political party must be subject to the party organizations in general, whether the party itself is working legally or illegally at the given moment. Communist nuclei of all kinds must be subordinated one to another in a strictly hierarchical order and system.

19. The Communist Party almost always begins its work among the industrial workers residing for the most part in cities. For the rapid victory of the working class it is necessary that the party should also work in the country, in the villages. The Communist Party must carry on its propaganda and organization work among the agricultural laborers and the poorer farmers. It must especially endeavor to organize Communist nuclei in the rural districts.

The international organization of the proletariat will be strong only if in all the countries where the Communists are carrying on their struggle the above principles of party organization and activity are firmly established. The Communist International invites to its Congress all labor unions which recognize the principles of the Third International, and are ready to break with the yellow International. The Communist International intends to organize an international section composed of the red labor unions, which recognize the principles of Communism. The Communist International will not refuse to co-operate with purely non-political workers' organizations desirous of carrying on a serious revolutionary struggle against the bourgeoisie. But at the same time the Communist International will never cease to emphasize to the workers of all the world:

1. The Communist International is the chief and essential instrument for the liberation of the working class. In each country there must now be not only Communist groups, or tendencies, but—a Communist Party.

2. In every country there must be only one Communist Party.

3. The Communist Party must be founded on the principle of the strictest centralization, and during the period of civil war it must introduce military discipline in its ranks.

4. In every place where there are a dozen proletarians or semi-proletarians, the Communist Party must have an organized nucleus.

5. In each non-political organization there must be a Communist nucleus, strictly subordinate to the party in general.

6. While firmly and faithfully supporting the program and revolutionary tactics of Communism, the Communist Party must always be closely united with the most widely spread workers' organizations and avoid sectarianism as much as lack of principle.

85

THE COMMUNIST PARTY
AND PARLIAMENTARISM

1. The New Epoch and the New Parliamentarism

THE ATTITUDE OF THE SOCIALIST PARTIES towards parliamentarism was originally, at the time of the First International, one of utilizing the bourgeois parliament for purposes of agitation. Participation in parliamentary activity was looked upon from the point of view of developing class consciousness, i. e., of awakening in the proletariat class hostility toward the ruling class. Changes in this attitude were brought about not through change of doctrine, but under the influence of political development. Owing to the uninterrupted advance of the forces of production and the widening sphere of capitalist exploitation, capitalism and together with it the parliamentary state acquired a lasting stability.

This gave rise to the adaptability of the parliamentary tactics of the Socialist parties to "organic" legislative activity in the bourgeois parliament, and the ever growing significance of the struggle for reforms within the capitalist system, as well as the predominating influence of the so-called "immediate demand" and the conversion of the maximum program into a figure of speech as an altogether remote "final goal." This served as a basis for the development of parliamentary careerism, corruption, and open or hidden betrayal of the fundamental interests of the working class.

The attitude of the Third International towards parliamentarism is determined not by a new doctrine, but by the changed goal of parliamentarism itself. During the previous epoch the parliament had performed a certain progressive function as the weapon of developing capitalism, but under the present conditions of unbridled imperialism, the parliament has become a tool of falsehood, deceit, violence and enervating chatter. In face of imperialistic devastation, plunder, violation, robbery and ruination, parliamentary reforms, devoid of system, of constancy and of definite plan, have lost every practical significance for the working masses.

Parliament has lost its stability like the whole of bourgeois society. The sudden transition from the organic to the critical epoch has created the foundation for new proletarian tactics in the field of parliamentarism. The Russian workers' party (Bolsheviks) have worked out the essence of revolutionary parliamentarism already in the preceding period, owing to the fact that Russia since 1905 has lost its political and social equilibrium and entered upon the period of storm and stress.

To the extent that some Socialists with an inclination for Communism point out that the moment of revolution in their respective countries has not yet arrived, and so decline to break away from the parliamentary opportunists, they reason in fact consciously or unconsciously from the consideration that the present epoch is one of relative stability for imperialist society, and they assume therefore that practical results may be achieved in the struggle for reform by a coalition with such men as Turatti and Longuet. But Communism based upon sound theoretical foundation must have a clear knowledge of the characteristics of present epoch (the culminations of capitalism, imperialistic self-negation and self-destruction, uninterrupted growth of civil war, etc.). Political relationships and political groupings may be different in different countries, but the essence of the matter is everywhere the same: we must start with the direct preparation of a proletarian uprising, politically and technically, for the destruction of the bourgeois state and for the creation of the new proletarian state.

The parliament at present can in no way serve as the arena of a struggle for reform, for improving the lot of the working people, as it was at certain periods of the preceding epoch. The centre of gravity of political life at present has been completely and finally transferred beyond the limits of the parliament. On the other hand, owing not only to its relationship to the working masses, but also to the complicated mutual relations within the various groups of the bourgeoisie itself, the bourgeoisie is forced to have some of its policies in one way or another passed through the parliament, where the various cliques haggle for power, exhibit their strong sides and betray their weak ones, get themselves unmasked, etc., etc. Therefore it is the immediate historical task of the working class to tear this apparatus out of the hands of the ruling classes, to break and destroy it, and to create in its place a new proletarian apparatus. At the same time, however, the revolutionary general staff of the working class is vitally concerned in having its scouting parties in the parliamentary institutions of the bourgeoisie in order to facilitate this task of destruction.

Thus the fundamental difference between the tactics of Communists entering parliament with revolutionary aims in view, and the tactics of the socialist parliamentarians, becomes perfectly clear. The latter act on the assumption of the relative stability and the indefinite durability of the existing order, they consider it their task to achieve reforms by all means and are concerned to make the masses appreciate every accomplishment as the merit of Social-Democratic parliamentarism (Turatti, Longuet and Co.).

Instead of the old compromising parliamentarism a new parliamentarism has come to life, as a weapon for the destruction of parliamentarism as a whole. But the aversion towards the traditional practices of the old parliamentarism drives some revolutionary elements into the camp of the opponents of parliamentarism on principle (I. W. W., the revolutionary Syndicalists, German Communist Labor Party).

Taking all this into consideration the Second Congress adopts the following theses:

2. Communism, the Struggle for the Dictatorship of the Proletariat, and the Utilization of the Bourgeois Parliament

1. Parliamentarism as a state system, has become a "democratic" form of the rule of the bourgeoisie, which at a certain stage of its development needs the fiction of national representation, that outwardly would be organization of a "national will" standing outside of classes, but in reality is an instrument of oppression and suppression in the hands of the ruling capitalists.

2. Parliamentarism is a definite form of the bourgeois State. Therefore it can in no way be a form of Communist society, which recognizes neither classes, nor class struggle, nor any form of the State.

3. Parliamentarism cannot be a form of proletarian government during the transition period between the dictatorship of the bourgeoisie and that of the proletariat. At the

moment when the intensified class struggle turns into civil war the proletariat must inevitably form its State organization as a fighting organization, which cannot admit any of the representatives of the former ruling classes; all fictions of a "national will" are harmful to the proletariat at this period, and a parliamentary division of authority is needless and injurious to it; the only form of proletarian dictatorship is a Republic of Soviets.

4. The bourgeois parliaments, which constitute one of the most important apparatus of the State machinery of the bourgeoisie, cannot be taken over by the proletariat any more than can the bourgeois order in general. The task of the proletariat consists in blowing up the whole machinery of the bourgeoisie, in destroying it, and all the parliamentary institutions with it, whether they be republican or constitutional-monarchy.

5. The same relates to the local government institutions of the bourgeoisie, which theoretically it is not correct to differentiate from State organizations. In reality they are part of the same apparatus of the State machinery of the bourgeoisie which must be destroyed by the revolutionary proletariat and replaced by local Soviets of Workers' Deputies.

6. Consequently, Communism repudiates parliamentarism as the form of the future; it renounces the same as a form of the class dictatorship of the proletariat; it repudiates the possibility of winning over the parliaments; its aim is to destroy parliamentarism. Therefore it is only possible to speak of utilizing the bourgeois State organizations with the object of destroying them. The question can only and exclusively be discussed on such a plane.

7. All class struggle is a political struggle, because it is finally a struggle for power. Any strike, when it spreads

through the whole country, is a menace to the bourgeois State, and thus acquires a political character. To strive to overthrow the bourgeoisie, and to destroy its State, means to carry on political warfare. To create working class apparatus—for the bridling and suppression of the resisting bourgeoisie—whatever such an apparatus may be, means to gain political power.

8. Consequently, the question of a political struggle is not identical with the attitude towards the parliamentary system. It is a general question of the class struggle of the proletariat, insofar as the struggle grows from a small to a general struggle for the overthrow of the capitalist order as a whole.

9. The fundamental means of the struggle of the proletariat against the rule of the bourgeoisie, that is, its state power, is, first of all, the method of mass demonstrations. Such mass demonstrations are prepared and carried out by the mass organizations of the proletariat, under the direction of a united, disciplined, centralized Communist Party. Civil war is war. In this war the proletariat must have its efficient political officers, its good political general staff, to conduct operations during all the stages of that fight.

10. The mass struggle means a whole system of developing activities growing ever more acute in form and logically leading to an uprising against the capitalist state. In this warfare of the masses developing into civil war, the guiding party of the proletariat must, as a general rule, secure every and all legal positions making them its auxiliaries in the revolutionary work, and subordinating such positions to the plans of the general campaign, that of the mass struggle.

11. One of such auxiliary supports is the rostrum of the bourgeois parliament. Against participation in a political campaign one should not use the argument that parliament

91

is a bourgeois government institution. The Communist Party enters such institutions not for the purpose of organization work, but in order to direct the masses to blow up the whole bourgeois machinery and the parliament itself from within (for instance, the work of Liebknecht in Germany, of the Bolsheviks in the Imperial Duma, in the "Democratic Conference," in the "Pre-parliament" of Kerensky, and lastly, in the "Constituent Assembly," and also in the Municipal Dumas, and the activities of the Bulgarian Communists).

12. This work within the parliaments, which consists chiefly in making revolutionary propaganda from the parliamentary platform, the denouncing of enemies, the ideological unification of the masses, who are still looking up to the parliamentary platform, captivated by democratic illusions, especially in backward territories, etc., must be fully subordinated to the objects and tasks of the mass struggle outside the parliaments.

The participation in the election campaign and the revolutionary propaganda from the parliamentary tribune has a special importance for the winning over of those strata of the workers, who—as perhaps the agrarian working masses— have stood far away from the revolutionary movement and the political life.

13. If the Communists have the majority in the local government institutions, they must: a) carry on a revolutionary opposition against the bourgeois central authority; b) do all for the aid of the poor population (economical measures, establishment or attempt to establish an armed workers' militia); c) point out on every occasion the barriers which the bourgeois State power puts against really great changes; d) develop on this basis the sharpest revolutionary propaganda without fearing a conflict with the State authorities;

92

e) under certain conditions substitute local Workers' Councils for the municipal administration. The whole activity of the Communists in the communal administration therefore must be a part of the general work of destruction of the capitalist system.

14. The election campaign must be carried on not for the purpose of obtaining a large number of seats in parliament, but for the revolutionary mobilization of the masses around the slogans of the proletarian revolution. The election campaign must be conducted by the entire mass of party members, not by the leaders alone; it is necessary to make use of and be in complete touch with all the manifestations of the masses (strikes, demonstrations, movements among the soldiers and sailors, etc.), going on at the moment; it is necessary to summon all the masses of the proletarian organizations to active work.

15. In complying with all these conditions, as well as with those indicated in a special instruction, the parliamentary work must present a direct contrast to the dirty "politics" which has been practiced by the Social Democratic parties of all countries, who enter parliament with the object of supporting that "democratic" institution or at best, to "win it over." The Communist Party can only recommend a revolutionary use of the parliament as exemplified by Karl Liebknecht, Heglund and the Bolsheviks.

3

16. "Anti-parliamentarism," in principle, in the sense of an absolute and categorical repudiation of participation in the elections and the parliamentary revolutionary work, cannot therefore bear criticism, and is a naive childish doctrine,

which is founded sometimes on a healthy disgust of politicians, but which does not understand the possibilities of revolutionary parliamentarism. Besides, very often this doctrine is connected with a quite erroneous representation of the role of the party, which in this case is considered not as a fighting, centralized advance guard of the workers, but as a decentralized system of badly joined revolutionary nuclei.

17. On the other hand, an acknowledgement of the value of parliamentary work in no wise leads to an absolute, in-all-and-any-case acknowledgement of the necessity of concrete elections and a concrete participation in parliamentary sessions. The matter depends upon a series of specific conditions. Under certain circumstances it may become necessary to leave the parliament. The Bolsheviks did so when they left the Pre-parliament in order to break it up, to weaken it, and to set up against it the Petrograd Soviet, which has then prepared to head the uprising; they acted in the same way in the Constituent Assembly on the day of its dissolution, converting the Third Congress of Soviets into the centre of political events. In other circumstances a boycotting of the elections may be necessary, and a direct violent storming of both the great bourgeois state apparatus and the parliamentary bourgeois clique, or a participation in the elections with a boycott of the parliament itself, etc.

18. In this way, while recognizing as a general rule the necessity of participating in the elections to the central parliament, and the institutions of local self-government, as well as in the work in such institutions, the Communist Party must decide the question concretely, according to the specific conditions of the given moment. Boycotting the elections or the parliament, or leaving the parliament, is permissible, chiefly when there is a possibility for an immediate transition to an armed fight for power.

94

19. At the same time one must constantly bear in mind the relative unimportance of this question. If the center of gravity lies in a struggle for the power outside the parliament, then naturally the question of a proletarian dictatorship and a mass fight for it is immeasurably greater than the secondary one of using the parliament.

20. Therefore the Communist International insists categorically that it considers any division or attempt at a division within the Communist parties, because of differences on this question, as a crime against the labor movement. The Congress calls upon all the elements which are in favor of the mass struggle for the proletarian dictatorship, under the direction of a centralized party of the revolutionary proletariat exercising its influence over all the mass-organizations of the working class—to strive for a complete unity between the Communist elements, notwithstanding any possible disagreement on the question of utilizing the bourgeois parliaments.

4. Revolutionary Parliamentarism

For securing the real execution of revolutionary parliamentary tactics it is necessary that:

1. The Communist Party in general and its Central Committee should, during the preparatory stage, before the parliamentary elections, inspect very carefully the quality of the personnel of the parliamentary factions. The Central Committee of the Communist Party should be responsible for the parliamentary Communist faction. The Central Committee shall have the undeniable right to reject any

candidate of any organization, if it is not perfectly convinced that such candidate will carry on a real Communist policy while in parliament.

The Communist parties must desist from the old Social-Democratic habit of electing as delegates only the so-called "experienced" parliamentarians, chiefly lawyers and so on. As a rule workmen should be put forward as candidates, without troubling about the fact that these may be sometimes simple rank-and-file workmen without much parliamentary experience. The Communist Party must treat with merciless contempt all elements who try to make a career by joining the party just before the elections in order to get into parliament. The Central Committees of Communist parties must sanction the candidacy of only such men who by long years of work have proved their unwavering loyalty to the working class.

2. When the elections are over, the organization of the parliamentary factions must be wholly in the hands of the Central Committee of the Communist Party—whether the party in general is a legal or illegal one at the given moment. The chairman and the bureau of the parliamentary faction of Communists must be confirmed in their functions by the Central Committee of the party. The central committee of the party must have its permanent representative in the parliamentary faction with the right of veto. On all important political questions the parliamentary faction shall get preliminary instructions from the central committee of the party.

At each forthcoming important debate of the Communists in the parliament, the Central Committee shall be entitled and bound to appoint or reject the orator of the faction, to demand that he submit previously the theses of his speech, or the text, for confirmation by the Central

Committee, etc. Each candidate entered in the list of the Communists must sign a paper to the effect that at the first request of the Central Committee of the party he shall be bound to give up his mandate, in order that in a given situation the act of leaving the parliament may be executed in unison.

3. In countries where reformists, semi-reformist, or simply career-seeking elements have managed to penetrate into the parliamentary faction of the Communists (as has already happened in several places), the central committees of the Communist parties are bound radically to weed out the personnel of the factions, on the principle that it is better for the cause of the working class to have a small but truly Communist faction, than a large one without a regular Communist line of conduct.

4. A Communist representative, by decision of the Central Committee, is bound to combine legal work with illegal work. In countries where the Communist delegate enjoys a certain inviolability, this must be utilized by way of rendering assistance to the illegal organizations and for the propaganda of the party.

5. The Communist representatives shall make all their parliamentary work dependent on the work of the party outside the parliament. The regular proposing of demonstrative measures, not for the purpose of having them passed by the bourgeois majority, but for the purposes of propaganda, agitation and organization, must be carried on under the direction of the party and its Central Committee.

6. In the event of labor demonstrations in the streets or other revolutionary movements, the Communist representatives must occupy the most conspicuous place—at the head of the proletarian masses.

7. The Communist representatives must try to get in

97

touch (under the control of the party) with the revolutionary workingmen, peasants and other workers either by
correspondence or otherwise. They must in no way act like
the Social Democratic deputies who carry on mere business
relations with their constituents. They must always be at
the disposal of the Communist organizations for propaganda work in the country.

8. Each Communist representative must remember that
he is not a "legislator," who is bound to seek agreements
with the other legislators, but an agitator of the party,
detailed into the enemy's camp in order to carry out the
orders of the party there. The Communist member is an-
swerable not to the wide mass of his constituents, but to his
own Communist party—whether legal or illegal.

9. The Communist representatives must speak in parliament in such a way as to be understood by every workman,
peasant, washer-woman, shepherd; so that the party may
publish his speeches and spread them to the most remote
villages of the country.

10. The rank-and-file Communist worker must not shrink
from speaking in the bourgeois parliaments, and not give
way to the so-called experienced parliamentarians, even if
such workmen are novices in parliamentary methods. In
case of need the workmen representatives may read their
speeches from notes, in order that the speech might be
printed afterwards in the papers or in leaflet form.

11. The Communist representative must make use of
the parliamentary tribune to denounce not only the bourgeoisie and its hangers-on, but also for the denunciation of
the social patriots, reformists, the half-and-half-politicians
of the centre and other opponents of Communism, and for
the wide propaganda of the ideas of the Third International.

12. The Communist representatives, even though there

98

should be only one or two of them in the parliament, should by their whole conduct challenge capitalism, and never forget that only those are worthy of the name of Communists, who not in words only but in deeds are the mortal enemy of the bourgeois order and its social-patriotic flunkeys.

THE TRADE UNION MOVEMENT
FACTORY COMMITTEES
AND THE THIRD INTERNATIONAL

THE TRADE UNIONS, created by the working class during the period of the peaceful development of capitalism, were organizations of the workers for the struggle for the increase of the price of labor at the labor market, and the improvement of labor conditions. The revolutionary Marxists endeavored by their influence to unite them with the political party of the proletariat, the Social Democracy, for a joint struggle for Socialism. For the same reasons that the international Social Democracy, with a few exceptions, proved to be not an instrument of the revolutionary struggle of the proletariat for the overthrow of capitalism, but an organization which held back the proletariat from revolution in the interests of the bourgeoisie, the trade unions proved to be in most cases, during the war, a part of the military apparatus of the bourgeoisie, helping the latter to extract from the working class as much sweat as possible for a more energetic warfare for capitalist profits. Containing chiefly the skilled workman, the better paid, limited by their craft narrowmindedness, fettered by a bureaucratic apparatus, which had removed itself from the masses, demoralized by their opportunist leaders, the labor unions betrayed not only the cause of the social revolution, but even also the struggle for the improvement of the conditions of life of the workmen organized by them. They relinquished the point of view of the trade union struggle against the employers, and replaced it by the program of an amiable arrangement with

100

the capitalists, at any cost. This policy was carried on not only by liberal unions of England and America, not only by the would-be "Socialist" trade unions in Germany and Austria, but by the Syndicalist unions in France as well.

2. The economic consequences of the war, the complete disorganization of world economy, the insane prices, the unlimited application of the labor of women and children, the aggravation of the housing conditions, all these are forcing the large masses of the proletariat into the struggle against capitalism. This struggle is revolutionary warfare, by its proportions, and by the character that it is assuming more and more every day; a warfare destroying objectively the bases of the capitalist order. The increase of wages, obtained one day by the economic struggle of one or another category of workers, is the next day nullified by the high prices. The prices must continue to rise, because the capitalist class of the victorious countries, ruining central and eastern Europe by their policy of exploitation, is not only not in a position to organize world economy, but is incessantly disorganizing it. For the success of their economic struggle the larger masses of workers who up to this time have stood apart from the labor unions, are now flowing into their ranks in a powerful stream. In all capitalist countries a tremendous increase of the trade unions is to be noticed, which now become organizations of the broad masses of the proletariat, not only of its advanced elements. Flowing into the unions, these masses strive to make them their weapons of battle. The sharpening of class antagonism compels the trade unions to lead strikes, which flow in a broad wave over the entire capitalist world, constantly interrupting the process of capitalist production and exchange. Increasing their demands in proportion to the rising prices and their own exhaustion, the working class undermine the bases of all

capitalist calculations that elementary premise of every well organized economic management. The unions, which during the war had been organs of influence and compulsion over the working masses, become in this way organs for the annihilation of capitalism.

3. The old trade union bureaucracy and the old forms of organization of the trade unions are in every way opposing and thwarting such a change in the nature of the trade unions. The old trade union bureaucracy is endeavoring in many places to maintain the trade unions as organizations of the workers' aristocracy, it preserves the rules which make it impossible for the badly paid working masses to enter into the trade union organizations. The old trade union bureaucracy is even now intensifying its efforts to replace the strike methods, which are ever more and more acquiring the character of revolutionary warfare between the bourgeoisie and the proletariat, by the policy of agreements with the capitalists, the policy of long-term contracts, which have lost all sense simply in view of the constant insane rise of prices. It tries to force upon the workers the policy of "Joint Industrial Councils," and to legally impede the leading of strikes with the assistance of the capitalist State. At the most tense moments of the struggle this bureaucracy sows dissention among the struggling masses of the workers, impeding unity of various categories of workmen into the general class struggle. In these attempts it is helped by the old organization of the trade unions according to crafts, which breaks up the workmen of one branch of production into separate trade groups, notwithstanding their being bound together by the process of capitalist exploitation. It rests on the force of tradition of the ideology of the old labor aristocracy, which is now constantly being weakened by the process of disintegration of the privilege of separate groups

of the proletariat through the general decay of capitalism, the equalization of the level of working class and the growth of its need and precariousness of its livelihood. In this way the trade union bureaucracy breaks up the powerful stream of the labor movement into weak streamlets, substitutes partial reformist demands for the general revolutionary aims of the movement, and on the whole retards the transformation of the struggle of the proletariat into a revolutionary struggle for the annihilation of capitalism.

4. Because of the rush of the enormous working masses into the trade unions, and also of the objective revolutionary character of the economic struggle which those masses are carrying on in spite of the trade union bureaucracy, the Communists must join such unions in all countries, in order to make of them efficient and conscious organs of the struggle for the abolition of capitalism and for Communism. They must initiate the forming of trade unions where these do not exist. All voluntary withdrawal from the economic movement, every artificial attempt to organize special unions, without being compelled thereto by exceptional acts of violence on the part of the trade union bureaucracy, such as expulsion of separate revolutionary local branches of the unions by the opportunist officials, or by their narrow-minded aristocratic policy, which prohibits the unskilled workers from entering into the organization, represents a great danger to the Communist movement. It threatens to isolate the most advanced, the most conscious workers from the masses, which are on the road to Communism, it threatens to hand over these masses to the opportunist leaders, playing into the hands of the bourgeoisie. . . . The hesitancy of the working masses, their ideological indecision, their tendency to yield to the arguments of opportunist leaders, can be overcome only during the process of the sharpening

struggle, by degrees, as the wider masses of the proletariat learn to understand, by experience, by their victories and defeats, that objectively it is already impossible to obtain human conditions of life on the basis of capitalist methods of management; and by degrees as the advanced Communist workmen learn through their economic struggle to be not only preachers of the ideas of Communism, but also the most determined leaders of the economic struggle and of the labor unions—only in this way will the Communists be able to take the lead of the trade union movement and make of it an organ of the revolutionary struggle for Communism. Only in this way can they prevent the break-up of the trade unions, and replace them by industrial unions—remove the old bureaucracy separated from the masses and replace it by the apparatus of shop delegates, leaving only the most routine functions to the central executive.

5. Placing the object and the essence of labor organizations higher than the form of organization, the Communists ought not to hesitate before a split in such organizations, if a refusal to split would mean abandoning revolutionary work in the trade unions, and giving up the attempt to make of them an instrument of revolutionary struggle, the attempt to organize the most exploited part of the proletariat. But even if such a split should be necessary, it must be carried into effect only at a time when the Communists have succeeded by the incessant warfare against the opportunist leaders and their tactics by their most active participation in the economic struggle, in persuading the wider masses of workmen that the split is occurring not because of the remote and as yet incomprehensible aims of the revolution, but on account of the concrete, immediate interests of the working class in the development of its economic struggle. The Communists in case a necessity for a split arises, must

continuously and attentively discuss the question as to whether such a split might not lead to their isolation from the working mass.

6. Where split between the opportunists and the revolutionary trade union movement has already taken place before, where, as in America, alongside of the opportunist trade unions there are unions with revolutionary tendencies —although not Communist ones—there the Communists are bound to support such revolutionary unions, to persuade them to abandon Syndicalist prejudices and to place themselves on the platform of Communism, which alone is a competent guide in the complicated problems of the economic struggle. Where within the trade unions or outside of them, in the factories, organizations are formed such as shop stewards, factory committees, etc., for the purpose of fighting against the counter-revolutionary tendencies of the trade union bureaucracy, to support the spontaneous direct action of the proletariat, there, of course, the Communists must with all their energy give assistance to these organizations. But the support of the revolutionary trade unions must not result in an exodus of Communists from the opportunist unions, which are in a state of ferment and beginning to recognize the class struggle. On the contrary, by acceleration of this evolution of the unions on their way to a revolutionary struggle, the Communists will be able to play the part of an element uniting the politically and economically organized workmen in their joint struggle for the abolition of capitalism.

The economic struggle of the proletariat becomes a political struggle during the epoch of the decline of capitalism much quicker than during the epoch of its peaceful development. Every serious economic clash may immediately place the workers face to face with the question of revolution.

Therefore it is the duty of the Communists in all the phases of the economic struggle to point out to the workers, that the success of the struggle is only possible if the working class conquers the capitalists in open fight, and by means of dictatorship proceeds to the organization of a Socialist order. Consequently, the Communists must strive to create as far as possible complete unity between the trade unions and the Communist Party, and to subordinate the unions to the leadership of the party, as the advanced guard of the workers' revolution. For this purpose the Communists should have Communist fractions in all the trade unions and factory committees and acquire by their means an influence over the labor movement and direct it.

2

1. The economic struggle of the proletariat for the increase of wages and the improvement of the conditions of life of the toiling masses, is getting more and more into a blind alley. The economic chaos, embracing one country after another in ever increasing proportions, is showing to even backward workmen that it is not enough to demand an increase of wages and a shortening of the working hours, and that the capitalist class is less capable every day of establishing the normal conditions of economic life and of guaranteeing to the workers at least those conditions of life which it gave them before the world war. Out of this growing conviction of the working masses are born their efforts to create organizations which will be able to commence a struggle for the alleviation of the situation by means of workers' control over production through the medium of the factory committees. This aspiration to create

factory committees, which is more and more taking possession of the workmen of different countries, takes its origin from the most varied causes (struggle against the counterrevolutionary bureaucracy, discouragement after union defeats, striving to create an organization embracing all workers) but at the end it results in the fight for control over industry, the special historic task of the factory committees. Therefore it is a mistake to form the factory committees only out of workmen who are already struggling for the dictatorship of the proletariat; on the contrary, the duty of the Communist Party is to organize all the workmen on the basis of the economic crisis, and to lead them toward the struggle for the dictatorship of the proletariat by developing the struggle for workers' control over production, which they all understand.

2. The Communist Party will be able to accomplish this task if, taking part in the struggle in the factory committees, it will instil into the minds of masses the consciousness that a systematic reconstruction of economic life on the basis of a capitalist order, which would mean its new enslavement by the State in favor of the capitalist class, is now totally impossible. The organization of the economic management corresponding with the interests of the working masses, is possible only when the state is in the hands of the working class, when the strong hand of the proletarian dictatorship will proceed to the abolition of capitalism and to the new Socialist organization.

3. The struggle of the factory committees against capitalism has for its immediate object workers' control over production.

The workers of every enterprise, every branch of industry, no matter what their trade, suffer from the "sabotage" of production on the part of capitalists, who frequently consider it more profitable to stop production in order that it might be easier to compel the workmen by the lash of starvation to agree to unsatisfactory labor conditions, or not to invest new capital in industry at a moment of a general rise in prices. The need to protect themselves against such sabotage of production by the capitalists unites the workmen independently of their political opinions, and therefore the factory committees elected by the workmen of a given enterprise are the broadest mass organizations of the proletariat. But the disorganization of capitalist management is the result not only of the conscious will of the capitalists, but in a still greater degree an inevitable decline of capitalism. Therefore in their struggle against the consequences of such a decline, the factory committees must go beyond the limits of control of separate factories. The factory committees of separate factories will soon be faced with the question of the workers' control over whole branches of industry and industry as a whole. And as any attempt on the part of the workmen to exercise a control over the supplying of the factories with raw material, or to control the financial operations of the factory owners, will meet with the most energetic measures against the working class on the part of the bourgeoisie and the capitalist government, the struggle for workers' control over production must lead to the struggle for seizure of power by the working class.

4. The campaign in favor of the factory committees must be conducted in such a way that into the minds of the masses, even not directly belonging to the factory proletariat, there should be instilled the conviction that the bourgeoisie is responsible for the economic crisis, while the proletariat, under the slogan of workers' control of industry, is struggling for the organization of production, for the suppression of speculation, disorganization and high prices. The duty of

the Communist Party is to struggle for control over production on the ground of the most critical questions of the day, the lack of fuel, the transport crisis—to unite the different groups of the proletariat and to attract wide circles of the petty bourgeoisie, which is being reduced to the status of proletarians day by day, and is suffering extremely from the economic crisis.

5. The factory committees cannot be substituted for the labor unions. During the process of struggle they may form unions outside the limits of single factories and trades, according to the branches of production, and create a general apparatus for the direction of the struggle. The labor unions are already now centralized fighting organs, although they do not embrace such wide masses of workmen as the factory committees are capable of, these latter being organizations which are accessible to all the workers of a given enterprise. The division of tasks between the factory committees and the labor unions is the result of the historical development of the social revolution. The labor unions organize the working masses for the struggle for the increase of wages and shortening of workhours on a national scale. The factory committees are organized for workers' control over production, for the struggle against the crisis, embracing all the workmen of the enterprises but their struggle can only gradually assume the character of a national one. The Communists must endeavor to transform the factory committees into the nuclei of the labor unions as soon as the unions overcome the counter-revolutionary tendencies of their bureaucracy, and when they consciously become organs of the revolution.

6. The duty of the Communists consists in inspiring the labor unions and the factory committees with a spirit of determined struggle, and the consciousness and knowledge

of the best methods of such a struggle—the spirit of Communism. In execution of this duty the Communists must practically subordinate the factory committees and the unions to the Communist Party, and thus create a proletarian mass organ, a basis for a powerful centralized party of the proletariat, embracing all the organizations of the proletarian struggle, leading them all to one aim, to the victory of the working class, through the dictatorship of the proletariat to Communism. The Communists converting the labor unions and factory committees into powerful weapons of the revolution, prepare these mass organizations for the great task which they will have after the establishment of the dictatorship of the proletariat, for the task of being the instrument of the reorganization of economic life on a Socialist basis. The labor unions, developed as industrial unions and supported by the factory committees as their factory organizations will then make the working masses acquainted with their tasks of production, they will educate the most experienced workmen to become leaders of the factories, to control the technical specialists, and together with the representatives of the Workers' State lay down the plan of the Socialist economic policy and carry it out.

3

1. The labor unions tried to form international unions, even in time of peace, because during strikes the capitalists used to invite workers from other countries as strike-breakers. But the International of Labor Unions had only a secondary importance before the war. It made one union support another when needful, it organized social statistics, but it did nothing for the organization of a joint struggle,

because the labor unions, under the leadership of opportunists, strove to avoid all revolutionary collisions on an
international scale. The opportunist leaders of the labor
unions, who each in his own country during the war was a
flunkey of his bourgeoisie are now striving to revive the
International of Labor Unions, attempting to make it a
weapon for the direct struggle of the international world
capital against the proletariat. Under the direction of Legien,
Jouhaux, Gompers, they are creating a Labor Bureau of the
League of Nations, that organization of international capitalist robbery. In all countries they are attempting to crush
the strike movement by means of laws, compelling the
workmen to submit to the arbitration of representatives of
the capitalist State.

They are endeavoring to obtain concessions for the skilled
workers by means of agreements with the capitalists, in
order to break in this way the growing unity of the working
class. The Amsterdam International of Labor Unions is
thus a substitute for the bankrupt Second International of
Brussels.

The Communist workers who are members of the labor
unions in all countries must on the contrary strive to create
an international battle front of labor unions. The question
now is not financial relief in case of strikes; but when a
danger is threatening the working class of one country, the
labor unions of the others, being organizations of the larger
masses, should all come to its defense; they should make it
impossible for the bourgeoisie of their respective countries
to render assistance to the bourgeoisie of the country engaged in the struggle against the working class. The economic struggle against the working class, the economic
struggle of the proletariat in all countries, is daily becoming
more and more a revolutionary struggle. Therefore the labor

111

unions must consciously use their forces for the support of all revolutionary struggles in their own and in other countries. For this purpose they must not only, in their own countries, strive to attain as great as possible centralization of their struggle, but they must do so on an international scale by joining the Communist International, and uniting into one army, the different parts of which shall carry on the struggle conjointly, supporting one another.

WHEN AND UNDER WHAT CONDITIONS
SOVIETS OF WORKERS' DEPUTIES
SHOULD BE FORMED

THE SOVIETS OF WORKERS' DEPUTIES appeared for the first time in Russia in 1905, at a time when the revolutionary movement of Russian workmen was at its height. Already in 1905 the Petrograd Soviet of Workers' Deputies was taking the first instinctive step towards a seizure of the power. And at that time the Petrograd Soviet was strong only as far as it had a chance of acquiring political power. As soon as the imperial counter-revolution rallied its forces and the labor movement slackened, the Soviet, after a short vegetation, ceased to exist.

2. When in 1916, at the beginning of a new strong revolutionary wave, the idea began to awaken in Russia regarding the immediate organization of Soviets of Workers' Deputies, the Bolshevik Party warned the workmen against the immediate formation of the Soviets, and pointed out that such a formation would be well-timed only at the moment when the revolution would have already begun and when the turn would have come for a direct struggle for the power.

3. At the beginning of the March Revolution of 1917, in Russia, when the Soviets of Workers' Deputies were transformed into Soviets of Workers' and Soldiers' Deputies, they drew into the sphere of their influence the widest circles of the masses and at once acquired a tremendous authority, because the real force was on their side, in their hands. But when the liberal bourgeoisie recovered from the suddenness of the first revolutionary blows, and when the social traitors, the Socialist-Revolutionaries and the Men-

sheviki helped the Russian bourgeoisie to take the power into its hands, the importance of the Soviets began to dwindle. Only after the July days and after the failure of Kornilov's counter-revolutionary campaign, when the broad masses began to move, and when the downfall of the counter-revolutionary bourgeois coalition government was apparent, then the Soviets began to flourish again; and they soon acquired a prominent importance in the country.

4. The history of the German and the Austrian revolution shows the same. When the masses revolted, when the revolutionary wave rose so high that it washed away the strongholds of the monarchies of the Hohenzollerns and the Hapsburgs, in Germany and in Austria the Soviets of Workers' and Soldiers' Deputies were formed with great rapidity. At first the real force was on their side, and the Soviets were well on the way to become the ruling power. But owing to a whole series of historical conditions, as soon as the power began to pass to the bourgeoisie and the counter-revolutionary Social-Democrats, then the Soviets began to decline and lose all importance. During the days of the unsuccessful counter-revolutionary revolt of Kapp-Lüttwitz in Germany, the Soviets again resumed their activity, but when the struggle ended again in the victory of the bourgeoisie and the social-traitors, the Soviets, which had just begun to revive, once more died away.

5. The above facts prove that for the formation of Soviets certain definite premises are necessary. To organize Soviets of Workers' Deputies, and transform them into Soviets of Workers' and Soldiers' Deputies, the following conditions are necessary:

a) A great revolutionary impulse among the widest circles of workmen and workwomen, the soldiers and the workers in general.

b) The acuteness of a political-economic crisis attaining such a degree that the power begins to slip out of the hands of the government;

c) When in the ranks of considerable masses of the workers and first of all when in the ranks of the Communist Party a serious determination to begin a systematic and regular struggle for the power has become ripe.

6. In the absence of these conditions the Communists may and should systematically and insistently propagate the idea of Soviets, popularize it among the masses, demonstrate to the widest circles of the population that the Soviets are the only efficient form of Government during the transition to complete Communism. But to proceed to a direct organization of Soviets in the absence of the above three conditions is impossible.

7. The attempt of the social traitors in Germany to project the Soviets into the general bourgeois-democratic constitutional system is treason to the workers' cause and deceit of the workmen. Real Soviets are possible only as a form of state organization, displacing bourgeois democracy, breaking it up and replacing it by a dictatorship of the proletariat.

8. The propaganda of the right leaders of the Independents (Hilferding, Kautsky, and others), who attempted to prove the compatibility of the "Soviet system" with the bourgeois Constituent Assembly, is either a complete misunderstanding of the laws of development of a proletarian revolution, or a conscious deceiving of the working class. The Soviets are the dictatorship of the proletariat. The Constituent Assembly is the dictatorship of the bourgeoisie. To unite and reconcile the dictatorship of the working class with that of the bourgeoisie is impossible.

9. The propaganda of some representatives of the Left Independents in Germany presenting the workers with a

ready-made plan of a "Soviet system," which has no relation whatever to the concrete process of the civil war is a doctrinaire pastime which draws the workers away from their essential tasks of the real struggle for power.

10. The attempts of separate Communist groups in France, Italy, America, England, to form Soviets not embracing the larger working masses and unable therefore to enter into a direct struggle for the power, are only prejudicial to the actual preparation of a Soviet revolution. Such artificial hot-house "Soviets" soon become transformed in the best of cases into small associations for propaganda of the idea of a Soviet power, and in the worst case such miserable "Soviets" are capable only of discrediting the idea of the power of "Soviets" in the eyes of the toiling masses.

11. At the present time there exists a special condition in Austria, where the working class has succeeded in preserving its Soviets, which unite large masses of workers. Here the situation resembles the period between February and October, 1917, in Russia. The Soviets in Austria represent a considerable political force, and appear to be the embryo of a new power.

It must be understood that in such a situation the Communists ought to participate in these Soviets, help the Soviets to penetrate into all phases of the social, economic, and political life of the country; they should create Communist factions within these Soviets, and by all means aid their development.

12. Soviets without a revolution are impossible. Soviets without a proletarian revolution inevitably become a parody of Soviets. The authentic Soviets of the masses are the historically revealed form of the dictatorship of the proletariat. All sincere and serious partisans of the power of Soviets should deal cautiously with the idea of Soviets and while

indefatigably propagating it among the masses, proceed to the direct realization of such Soviets only under the conditions mentioned above.

THESES ON THE NATIONAL
AND COLONIAL QUESTIONS

A. Theses

IT IS TYPICAL of bourgeois democracy by its very nature, to take an abstract or formal attitude towards the question of the colonies in general, and to that of national equality in particular. Under the slogan of the equality of human beings in general, bourgeois democracy proclaims the formal or juridical equality of the proprietor and the proletarian, of the exploiter and the exploited, thereby greatly deceiving the oppressed classes. On the pretext of absolute equality of human beings, the bourgeoisie converts the idea of equality which is in itself but a reflection of the relations caused by commodity production, into an instrument of the struggle against the abolition of classes. But the real essence of the demand for equality is based on the demand for the abolition of classes.

2. In conformity with its chief task—the struggle against bourgeois democracy and the denunciation of its lies and deceptions the Communist Party, being the class conscious expression of the struggle of the proletariat to cast off the yoke of the bourgeoisie, must not advance any abstract and formal principles on the national question, but must first analyze the historical and, before all, the economic conditions; second, it must clearly distinguish the interests of the oppressed classes, of the toilers, of the exploited from the general conception of national interests which in reality means the interests of the ruling class; third, it must equally

118

separate the oppressed and subject nations from the dominating nations, in contradistinction to the bourgeois democratic lies concealing the enslavement of a vast majority of the population of the earth by an insignificant minority of the advanced capitalist nations, which is peculiar to the epoch of financial capital and imperialism.

3. The imperialist war of 1914-1918 has demonstrated very clearly to all nations and to all oppressed classes of the world the deceitfulness of bourgeois democratic phraseology. This war has been carried on on both sides under the false slogan of the freedom of nations and national self-determination. But the Brest-Litovsk and Bucharest peace on the one hand, and the Versailles and Saint Germain peace on the other, have shown how the bourgeoisie establishes even "National" boundaries in conformity with its own economic interests. "National" boundaries are for the bourgeoisie nothing but market commodities. The so-called "League of Nations" is nothing but an insurance policy in which the victors mutually guarantee each other their prey. The striving for the reconstruction of national unity and of the "reunion of alienated territories" on the part of the bourgeoisie is nothing but an attempt of the vanquished to gather forces for new wars. The reuniting of the nationalities artificially torn asunder corresponds also to the interests of the proletariat, but real national freedom and unity can be achieved by the proletariat only through revolutionary struggle and by the overthrow of the bourgeoisie. The League of Nations and the entire policy of the imperialist powers after the war demonstrate this even more clearly and definitely, making the revolutionary struggle in the advanced countries more acute, increasing the ferment of the working masses of the colonies and the subject countries, and dispelling the middle class nationalistic illusion

of the possibility of peaceful collaboration and equality of nations under capitalism.

4. It follows from the fundamental principles laid down above, that the policy of the Communist International on the national and colonial questions must be chiefly to bring about a union of the proletarian and working masses of all nations and countries for a joint revolutionary struggle leading to the overthrow of landowners and capitalists. For only such a union can assure the victory over capitalism, without which national inequality and oppression cannot be abolished.

5. The political situation of the world at the present time has placed the question of the dictatorship of the proletariat in the foreground, and all the events of world politics are inevitably concentrating around one point, namely, the struggle of the bourgeois world against the Russian Soviet Republic, which is grouping around itself the Soviet movements of the vanguard of the workers of all countries, and all national liberation movements of the colonial and subject countries, which have been taught by bitter experience that there can be no salvation for them outside of a union with the revolutionary proletariat, and the triumph of the Soviet power over imperialism.

6. Consequently, we must not content ourselves with a mere recognition or declaration concerning the unity of the workers of different nations, but we must carry out a policy of realizing the closest union between all national and colonial liberation movements and Soviet Russia, determining the forms of this union in accordance with the stage of development of the Communist movement among the proletariat of each country or the nationalist revolutionary liberation movement in the subject nations and backward countries.

7. Federation is a transitional form towards the complete union of the workers of all countries. It has already proved its efficiency in practice in the relations of the Socialist Federated Soviet Republic of Russia to the other Soviet Republics (Hungarian, Finnish, Lettish, in the past, and the Azerbeidjan and Ukrainian in the present), as also within the borders of the Socialist Federal Soviet Republic of Russia with regard to the nationalities which had neither their own government nor any self-governing institutions (for example, the autonomous Republic of Bashkiria and the Tartar Republic, which were formed in 1919-1920 by the Russian Socialist Federated Soviet Republic).

8. It is the task of the Communist International in this regard not only to further develop, but also to study and test by experience, these federations which have arisen out of the Soviet order and the Soviet movement. Recognizing federation as a transitional form towards complete union, we must strive for ever closer federative connections, bearing in mind first the impossibility of maintaining the Soviet Republic surrounded by powerful imperialist nations, without a close union with other Soviet Republics; second, the necessity of a close economic union of the Soviet Republics, without which the restoration of the forces of production destroyed by imperialism and the assuring of the welfare of the workers is impossible; third, the striving towards the creation of a unified world economy based on one general plan and regulated by the proletariat of all the nations of the world. This tendency has already manifested itself under capitalism, and is undoubtedly going to be further developed and perfected by Socialism.

9. With regard to inter-state relations, the international policy of the Communist International cannot limit itself to a mere formal, meaningless declaration of the recognition

of the equality of nations, which does not comprise practical obligations, such as has been made by the bourgeois democrats who come out openly as such or who call themselves "socialists." The constant violations of the equality of nations and the infringement upon the rights of national minorities practised in all the capitalist states in spite of their democratic constitutions, must be denounced in all the propaganda and agitational activity of the Communist parties within as well as outside of the parliament. It is likewise necessary, first, to explain constantly that only the Soviet regime is able to give the nations real equality, by uniting the proletariat and all the masses of the workers in the struggle against the bourgeoisie; second, to support the revolutionary movement among the subject nations and those deprived of equal rights (for example: Ireland, American negroes, etc.), and in the colonies directly through the Communist parties.

Without this last especially important condition, the struggle against the oppression of dependent nations and colonies, as well as the recognition of their right to an independent existence, is only a misleading signboard, such as has been exhibited by the parties of the Second International.

10. It is the habitual practice not only of the centre parties of the Second International, but also of those which have left it, to recognize internationalism in words and then to adulterate it in their propaganda, agitation and practical activity by mixing it up with petty bourgeois nationalism and pacifism. This is to be found even among those parties that at present call themselves Communist. The struggle against this evil, and against the deep-rooted petty bourgeois national prejudices (manifesting themselves in various forms, such as race hatred, national antagonism and anti-

semitism), must be brought to the foreground the more vigorously because of the urgent necessity of transforming the dictatorship of the proletariat and changing it from a national basis (i. e., existing in one country and incapable of exercising an influence over world politics), into an international dictatorship (i. e., a dictatorship of the proletariat of at least several advanced countries capable of exercising a determined influence upon world politics). Petty bourgeois nationalism considers internationalism to mean the mere recognition of the rights of national equality, and preserves intact national egotism—disregarding its mere verbal recognition. Proletarian internationalism on the other hand demands: 1) the subordination of the interests of the proletarian struggle in one country to the interests of that struggle on an international scale; 2) the capability and readiness on the part of one nation which has gained a victory over the bourgeoisie, of making the greatest national sacrifices for the overthrow of international capitalism.

In the countries in which fully developed capitalist states exist, the labor parties comprising the vanguard of the proletariat must consider it as their primary and most important task to combat the opportunist and petty bourgeois pacifist confusion of the ideas and the policy of internationalism.

11. With regard to those states and nationalities where a backward, mainly feudal, patriarchal, or patriarchal-agrarian regime prevails, the following must be borne in mind: 1) All Communist parties must give active support to the revolutionary movements of liberation, the form of support to be determined by a study of existing conditions, carried on by the party wherever there is such. This duty of rendering active support is to be imposed, in the first place, on the workers of those countries on whom the sub-

ject nation is dependent in a colonial or financial way; 2) Naturally a struggle must be carried on against the reactionary mediaeval influences of the clergy, the Christian missions and similar elements; 3) It is also necessary to combat the pan-Islam and pan-Asiatic and similar movements, which are endeavoring to utilize the liberation struggle against European and American imperialism for the purpose of strengthening the power of Turkish and Japanese imperialists, of the nobility, of the large landowners, of the clergy, etc.; 4) It is of special importance to support the peasant movements in backward countries against the landowners and all feudal survivals; above all we must strive as far as possible to give the peasant movement a revolutionary character, to organize the peasants and all the exploited into the Soviets, and thus bring about the closest possible union between the Communist proletariat of Western Europe and the revolutionary peasant movement of the East and of the colonial and backward countries; 5) It is likewise necessary to wage determined war against the attempt of the quasi-Communist revolutionists to cloak the liberation movement in the backward countries with a Communist garb. It is the duty of the Communist International to support the revolutionary movement in the colonies and in the backward countries, for the exclusive purpose of uniting the various units of the future proletarian parties —such as are Communists not only in name—in all backward countries and educate them to the consciousness of their specific tasks, i. e., to the tasks of the struggle against the bourgeois democratic tendencies within their respective nationalities. The Communist International must establish temporary relations and even unions with the revolutionary movements in the colonies and backward countries, without however amalgamating with them, but preserving the independent character of the proletarian movement even though it be still in its embryonic state. 6) It is essential to continually expose the deception fostered among the masses of the toilers in all, and especially in the backward countries, by the imperialist powers aided by the privileged classes of the subject countries, in creating under the mask of political independence various governments and state institutions which are in reality completely dependent upon them economically, financially and in a military sense. As a striking example of the deception practised upon the working class of a subject country through the combined efforts of Allied imperialism and the bourgeoisie of the given nation, we may cite the Palestine affair of the Zionists, where under the pretext of creating a Jewish state in Palestine, in which the laboring Jews form only an insignificant part of the population, Zionism has delivered the native Arabian working population to the exploitation of England. Only a union of Soviet Republics can bring salvation to the dependent and weak nationalities under present international conditions.

12. The age-long enslavement of the colonial and weak nationalities by the imperialist powers, has given rise to a feeling of rancor among the masses of the enslaved countries, as well as to a feeling of distrust towards the oppressing nations in general and towards the proletariat of those nations. These sentiments have become strengthened by the base treachery to Socialism of the majority of the official leaders of the proletariat in the years of 1914-1919, when the social patriots came out in defence of their fatherlands and of the "rights" of their bourgeoisie to the enslavement of the colonies and to the plunder of the financially dependent countries. These sentiments can be completely rooted out only by the abolition of imperialism in the advanced coun-

tries and the radical transformation of all the foundations of economic life in the backward countries. Thus it will take a long time for these national prejudices to disappear. This imposes upon the class-conscious Communist proletariat of all countries the duty of exercising special caution and care with regard to these national sentiments still surviving in the countries and nationalities which have been subjected to lasting enslavement, and also of making necessary concessions in order more speedily to remove this distrust and prejudice. The victory over capitalism cannot be fully achieved and carried to its ultimate goal unless the proletariat and the toiling masses of all nations of the world rally of their own accord in a concordant and close union.

B. Supplementary Theses

1. To determine more especially the relation of the Communist International to the revolutionary movements in the politically subjected countries with a pre-capitalist order, for instance, China and India, is one of the most important questions before the Second Congress of the Third International. The history of the world revolution has come to a period when a proper understanding of this relation is indispensable. The great European war and its results have shown clearly that the masses of non-European subjected countries are inseparably connected with the proletarian movement in Europe, as a consequence of the centralization of world capitalism—for instance, the sending of colonial troops and huge armies of workers to the battlefront during the war, etc.

2. One of the main sources from which European capitalism draws its chief strength is to be found in the colonial possessions and dependencies. Without the control of the extensive markets and vast fields of exploitation in the colonies, the capitalist powers of Europe cannot maintain their existence even for a short time. England, the stronghold of imperialism has been suffering from overproduction since more than a century ago. But for the extensive colonial possessions acquired for the sale of her surplus products and as a source of raw materials for her ever-growing industries, the capitalist structure of England would have been crushed under its own weight long ago. By enslaving the hundreds of millions of inhabitants of Asia and Africa, English imperialism succeeds in keeping the British proletariat under the domination of the bourgeoisie.

3. Super-profit gained in the colonies is the mainstay of the modern capitalism, and so long as the latter is not deprived of this source of super-profit, it will not be easy for the European working-class to overthrow the capitalist order. Thanks to the possibility of the extensive and intensive exploitation of human labor and natural resources in the colonies, the capitalist nations of Europe are trying not without success, to recuperate their present bankruptcy. By exploiting the masses in the colonies, European imperialism will be in a position to give concession after concession to the labor aristocracy at home. Whilst on the one hand, European imperialism seeks to lower the standard of living of the home proletariat by bringing into competition the productions of the lower paid workers in subject countries, on the other hand, it will not hesitate to go to the extent of sacrificing the entire profit in the home country so long as it continues to gain its huge super-profits in the colonies.

4. The breaking up of the colonial empire, together with

the proletarian revolution in the home country, will over-throw the capitalist system in Europe. Consequently, the Communist International must widen the sphere of its activities. It must establish relations with those revolutionary forces that are working for the overthrow of imperialism in the countries subjected politically and economically. These two forces must be co-ordinated if the final success of the world revolution is to be guaranteed.

5. The Communist International is the concentrated will of the world revolutionary proletariat. Its mission is to organize the working class of the whole world for the overthrow of the capitalist order and the establishment of Communism. The Third International is a fighting body which must asume the task of combining the revolutionary forces of all the countries of the world. Dominated as it was by a group of politicians, permeated with bourgeois culture, the Second International failed to appreciate the importance of the colonial question. For them the world did not exist outside of Europe. They could not see the necessity of co-ordinating the revolutionary movement of Europe with those in the non-European countries. Instead of giving moral and material help to the revolutionary movement in the colonies, the members of the Second International themselves became imperialists.

6. Foreign imperialism, imposed on the Eastern peoples prevented them from developing, socially and economically and reaching the same stage of development as the people of Europe and America. Owing to the imperialist policy of preventing industrial development in the colonies, a proletarian class, in the strict sense of the word, could not come into existence there until recently. The indigenous craft industries were destroyed to make room for the products of the centralized industries in the imperialistic countries—

consequently a majority of the population was driven to the land to produce food grains and raw materials for export to foreign lands. On the other hand, there followed a rapid concentration of land in the hands of the big landowners of financial capitalists and the state, thus creating a huge landless peasantry. The great bulk of the population was kept in a state of illiteracy. As a result of this policy, the spirit of revolt latent in every subject people, found its expression only through the small, educated middle class.

Foreign domination has obstructed the free development of the social forces, therefore its overthrow is the first step towards a revolution in the colonies. Thus to help to overthrow the foreign rule in the colonies is not to indorse the nationalist aspirations of the native bourgeoisie, but to open the way to the liberation of the smothered proletariat there.

7. There are to be found in the dependent countries two distinct movements which every day grow farther apart from each other. One is the bourgeois democratic nationalist movement, with a program of political independence under the bourgeois order, and the other is the mass action of the poor and ignorant peasants and workers for their liberation from all sorts of exploitation. The former endeavor to control the latter, and often succeed to a certain extent, but the Communist International must struggle against such control and help to develop class consciousness in the working masses of the colonies. The first step towards revolution in the colonies must be the overthrow of foreign capitalism.

But the foremost and necessary task is the formation of the non-party organization of peasants and workers for the purpose of leading them to the revolution and to the establishment of Soviet republics. Thus the masses in the backward countries may reach Communism, not through capitalistic development, but led by the class conscious proletariat of the advanced countries.

8. The real strength of the liberation movements in the colonies is no longer confined to the narrow circle of bourgeois-democratic nationalists. In most of the colonies there already exist organized revolutionary parties which strive to be in close connection with the working masses. (The relation of the Communist International with the revolutionary movement in the colonies should be realized through the mediums of these parties or groups, because they were the vanguard of the working class in their respective countries.) They are not very large to-day, but they reflect the aspirations of the masses and the latter will follow them to the revolution. The Communist parties of the different imperialistic countries must work in conjunction with these proletarian parties of the colonies, and through them, give all moral and material support to the revolutionary movement in general.

The revolution in the colonies is not going to be a Communist revolution in its first stages. But if from the outset the leadership is in the hands of a Communist vanguard, the revolutionary masses will not be led astray, but may go ahead through the successive periods of development of revolutionary experience. Indeed it would be extremely erroneous in many of the Oriental countries, to try to solve the agrarian problem, according to pure Communist principles. In its first stages, the revolution in the colonies must be carried on with a program which will include many petty bourgeois reform clauses, such as division of land, etc. But from this it does not follow at all that the leadership of the revolution will have to be surrendered to the bourgeois democrats. On the contrary, the proletarian parties must carry on vigorous and systematic propaganda of the Soviet idea and organize the peasants' and workers' Soviets as soon as possible. These Soviets will work in co-operation with the Soviet republics in the advanced capitalist countries for the ultimate overthrow of the capitalist order throughout the world.

THESES
ON THE AGRARIAN QUESTION

N ONE BUT THE CITY INDUSTRIAL PROLETARIAT, led by
the Communist Party, can emancipate the laboring
masses in the country from the yoke of capital and
landlordism, from ruin and from imperialistic wars, inevitable as long as the capitalist system endures. There is no salvation for the peasants except to join the Communist proletariat, to support with heart and soul its revolutionary
struggle to throw off the yoke of the landlords and the
bourgeoisie.

On the other hand the industrial workers will be unable
to carry out their universal historic mission, and to liberate
humanity from the bondage of capital and war, if they shut
themselves within their separate crafts, their narrow trade-
union interests, and restrict themselves self-sufficiently to a
desire for the improvement of their sometimes tolerable
petty bourgeois conditions of life. That is what happens in
most advanced countries possessing a "labor aristocracy,"
which forms the basis of the would-be Socialist parties of the
Second International, who are in fact the worst enemies of
Socialism, traitors to it, petty bourgeois jingoes, agents of
the bourgeoisie in the labor movement. The proletariat
becomes a truly revolutionary class, truly Socialist in its
actions, only by acting as the vanguard of all those who •
work and are being exploited as their leader in the struggle
for the overthrow of the oppressors; and this cannot be
achieved without carrying the class struggle into the agricultural districts, without making the laboring masses of
the country all gather around the Communist Party of the

town proletariat without the peasants' being educated by the town proletariat.

2. The laboring and exploited masses in the country, which the town proletariat must lead on to the fight or at least win over on its side, are represented in all capitalist countries by the following groups:

In the first place the agricultural proletariat, the hired laborers (by the year, by the day, by the job), making their living by wage labor in capitalist, agricultural or industrial establishments. The independent organization of this class, separated from the other groups of the country population (in a political, military, trade, co-operative, educational sense), and an energetic propaganda among it, in order to win it over to the side of the Soviet power and of the dictatorship of the proletariat—such is the fundamental task of the Communist parties in all countries.

In the second place the semi-proletariat or small peasants, those who make their living partly by working for wages in agricultural and industrial capitalist establishments, partly by toiling on their own or a rented parcel of land yielding but a part of the necessary food produce for their families. This class of the rural population is rather numerous in all capitalist countries, but its existence and its peculiar position is hushed up by the representatives of the bourgeoisie and the yellow "Socialists" affiliated to the Second International. Some of these people intentionally cheat the workers, but others follow blindly the average views of the public and mix up this special class with the whole mass of the "peasantry." Such a method of bourgeois deceit of the workers is used more particularly in Germany and France, and then in America and other countries. Provided that the work of the Communist Party is well organized, this group is sure to side with the Communists, the conditions of life of these half-proletarians being very hard, the advantage the Soviet power and the dictatorship of the proletariat would bring them being enormous and immediate. In some countries there is no clear cut distinction between these two groups; it is therefore permissible under certain conditions to form them into separate organizations.

In the third place the little proprietors, the small farmers who possess by right of ownership or on rent small portions of land which satisfy the needs of their family and of their farming without requiring any additional wage labor. This part of the population as a class gains everything by the victory of the proletariat, which brings with it: a) liberation from the payment of rent or of a part of the crops (for instance the metayers in France, the same arrangements in Italy, etc.) to the owners of large estates; b) Abolition of all mortgages; c) Abolition of many forms of pressure and of dependence on the owners of large estates (forests and their use, etc.); d) Immediate help from the proletarian state for farm work (permitting use by peasants of the agricultural implements and partly the buildings on the big capitalist estates expropriated by the proletariat, immediate transformation by the proletarian state power of all rural cooperatives and agricultural companies, which under the capitalist rule were chiefly supporting the wealthy and the middle peasantry, into institutions primarily for support of the poor peasantry, that is to say, the proletarians, semi-proletarians, small farmers, etc.).

At the same time the Communist Party should be thoroughly aware that during the transitional period leading from capitalism to Communism, i. e., during the dictatorship of the proletariat, at least some partial hesitations are inevitable in this class in favor of unrestricted commerce and free use of the rights of private property. For this class,

134

being a seller of commodities (although on a small scale),
is necessarily demoralized by profit-hunting and habits of
proprietorship. And yet provided there is a consistent proletarian policy, and the victorious proletariat deals relentlessly with the owners of the large estates and landed peasants, the hesitations of the class in question will not be
considerable, and cannot change the fact that on the whole
this class will side with the proletarian revolution.

3. All these three groups taken together constitute the
majority of agrarian population in all capitalist countries.
This guarantees in full the success of the proletarian revolution, not only in the towns but in the country as well. The
opposite view is very widely spread, but it persists only
because of a systematic deceit on the part of bourgeois
science and statistics. They hush up by every means any
mention of the deep chasm which divides the rural classes
we have indicated, from the exploiters, the landowners and
capitalists, as well as the half-proletarians and small peasants
on the one hand, from the landed peasants on the other.
It holds further because of the incapacity and the failure
of the heroes affiliated to the yellow Second International
and the "labor aristocracy," demoralized by imperialistic
privileges, to do genuine propaganda and organization work
for the benefit of the proletarian revolution, and agitation
among the poor in the country. All the attention of the
opportunists was given and is being given now to the arrangement of theoretical and practical agreements with the bourgeoisie, including the landed and the middle peasantry, and
not to the revolutionary overthrow of the bourgeois government and the bourgeois class by the proletariat. In the third
place, this view persists because of the force of inveterate
prejudice possessing already a great stability (and connected
with all bourgeois-democratic and parliamentary prej-

udices), the incapacity to grasp a simple truth fully proved by the Marxian theory and confirmed by the practice of the proletarian revolution in Russia. This truth consists in the fact that the peasant population of the three classes we have mentioned above, with the exception of the agricultural laborers who are already on the side of the revolution, being extremely oppressed, scattered and doomed to live in half-civilized conditions in all countries, even in the most advanced, is economically, socially, and morally interested in the victory of socialism; but that it will finally support the revolutionary proletariat only after the proletariat has taken the political power, after it has done away with the owners of the large estates and the capitalists, after the oppressed masses are able to see in practice that they have an organized leader and helper sufficiently powerful and firm to support and to guide, to show the right way.

4. The "middle peasantry," in the economic sense consists, of small landowners who possess, by the right of ownership or rent, portions of land, which, although small, nevertheless may yield usually under capitalist rule not only a scanty provision for the family and the needs of the farming, but also the possibility of accumulating a certain surplus, which, at least in the best years, could be transformed into capital; and which need to employ (for instance in a family of two or three members) wage labor. As a concrete example of the middle peasantry in an advanced capitalist country we may take Germany, according to the registration of 1917, a group with farms from twelve to twenty-five acres, and in which farms the number of farms employing laborers makes up about a third of the whole number of farms in this group.* In France, the country of greater development of

*These are the exact figures: Number of farms from 5-10 acres 552,798 out of 5,736,082; they possess all sorts of hired workers,

special cultures, for instance the vine-yards, requiring special treatment and care, the corresponding group employs wage labor probably in a somewhat larger proportion.

The revolutionary proletariat can not make it its aim, at least for the nearest future, and for the beginning of the period of the proletarian dictatorship to win this group over to its side. The proletariat will have to content itself with neutralizing this group, i. e., with making it take a neutral position in the struggle between the proletariat and the bourgeoisie. The vacillation of this group is unavoidable, and in the beginning of the new epoch its predominating tendency in the advanced capitalist countries will be in favor of the bourgeoisie, for the ideas and sentiments of owners of private property are predominant here. The victorious proletariat will immediately improve the lot of this group by abolishing the system of rent and mortgage, by the introduction of machinery and electrical appliances in agricultural production, putting the peasants in possession of the land they used to rent (abolition of rents). The proletarian State power cannot at once abolish private property in most of the capitalist countries, but must do away with all duties and levies imposed upon this class of people by the landlords; it will also secure to the small and middle peasantry the ownership of their landholdings, and enlarge them.

The combination of such measures together with a relentless struggle against the bourgeoisie guarantees the full success of the neutralization policy. The transition to collective agriculture must be managed with much circumspection

487,704; the number of workers with their families (*Familienangehoerige*) being 2,013,633. In Austria, according to the census of 1910, there were 383,351 farms in this group: 126,136 of them employing hired labor; 146,044 hired workers, 1,215,969 workers with their families. The total number of farms in Austria amounts to 2,856,349.

137

and step by step, and the proletarian state power must realize by the force of example the introduction of technical improvements without any voilence toward the middle peasantry.

5. The landed peasants or farmers are capitalists in agriculture, managing their lands usually with several hired laborers. They are connected with the "peasantry" only by their rather low standard of culture, their way of living, their personal manual work of their land. This is the most numerous element of the bourgeois class, and the decided enemy of the revolutionary proletariat. The chief attention of the Communist Party in the rural districts must be given to the struggle against this element, to the liberation of the laboring and exploited majority of the rural population from the moral and political influence of these exploiters.

After the victory of the proletariat in the towns this class will inevitably oppose it by all means, from sabotage to open armed counter-revolutionary resistance. The revolutionary proletariat must therefore immediately begin to prepare the necessary force for the disarming of every single man of this class, and together with the overthrow of the capitalists in industry, the proletariat must deal a relentless crushing blow to this class. To that end it must arm the rural proletariat and organize soviets in the country, with no room for exploiters and a preponderant place reserved to the proletarians and the semi-proletarians.

But the expropriation even of the landed peasants can by no means be an immediate object of the victorious proletariat, considering the lack of material, particularly of technical material and further of the social conditions necessary for the socialization of such lands. In some probably exceptional cases parts of their estates will be confiscated if they are leased in small parcels, or if they are specially needed by

138

the small-peasant population. A free use must be also secured to this population, on definite terms, of a part of the agricultural machinery of the landed peasants, etc. As a general rule, however, the state power must leave the peasants in possession of their land, confiscating it only in case of resistance to the government of the laboring and exploited peasants. The experience of the Russian proletarian revolution, whose struggle against the landed peasants became very complicated and prolonged owing to a number of special circumstances, nevertheless shows that this class has been at last taught what it costs to make the slightest attempt at resistance, and is now quite willing to serve loyally the aims of the proletarian state. It begins even to be penetrated, although very slowly, by a respect for the government which protects every worker and deals relentlessly with the idle rich.

The specific conditions which complicated and prolonged the struggle of the Russian proletariat against the landed peasantry after the overthrow of the bourgeoisie, consisted mainly in the fact that after the coup d'état of October 25-November 7, 1917, the Russian revolution traversed a stage of "general democratic," actually bourgeois democratic, struggle of the peasantry as a whole against the landowners, in the low standard of culture and the numerical weakness of the town-proletariat, and finally the enormous distances and exceedingly bad transport conditions. As far as these adverse conditions do not exist in the advanced countries, the revolutionary proletariat in Europe and America must prepare with much more energy and carry out a much more rapid and complete victory over the resistance of the landed peasantry depriving it of all possibility of resistance. This is of the utmost importance, considering that until a complete, absolute victory is won, the village proletarians, semi-proletarians and small peasants will not recognize the state power of the proletariat as solid and secure.

6. The revolutionary proletariat must proceed to an immediate and unconditional confiscation of the estates of the landowners and big landlords, that is of all those who systematically employ wage labor, directly or through their tenants, exploiting all the small (and not infrequently also the middle) peasantry in their neighborhood, and do not do any actual manual work. To this element belong the majority of the descendants of the feudal lords (the nobility of Russia, Germany and Hungary, the restored seigneurs of France, the Lords in England, the former slave owners in America) or financial magnates who have become particularly rich, or a mixture of those two classes of exploiters and idlers.

No propaganda can be permitted in the ranks of the Communist parties in favor of an indemnity to be paid to the owners of large estates for their expropriation. In the present conditions prevailing in Europe and America this would mean a treason to Socialism and the imposition of a new tax on the laboring and exploited masses, who have already suffered from the war—which has increased the number of millionaires and multiplied their wealth.

In the advanced capitalist countries the Communist International considers that it should be a prevailing practice to preserve the large agricultural establishments and manage them on the lines of the "Soviet farms" in Russia.* In regard to the management of the estates confiscated by the victorious proletariat from the owners of large landed property, the prevailing practice in Russia, the cause of economic backwardness, was that of the partition of this

*It is also advisable to encourage collective establishments (Communes).

landed property for the benefit of the peasantry, and comparatively rare exceptions were the preservation of the so-
called "Soviet farm," managed by the proletarian state at its
expense, and transforming the former wage laborers into
workers employed by the state, and into members of the
Soviets managing these farms.

The preservation of large landholdings serves best the
interests of the revolutionary elements of the population,
namely the landless agricultural workers and semi-proletarian small landholders, who get their livelihood mainly by
working in the large estates. Besides, the nationalization of
large landholdings makes the urban population at least in
part, less dependent on the peasantry for their food.

In those places, however, where relics of the feudal system
still prevail, the landlord privileges give rise to special forms
of exploitation, where "serfdom" and the system of giving
half of the products to the landlord still prevail, there under
certain conditions it becomes necessary to transfer to the
peasants a part of the soil belonging to the large estates.

In countries where large landholdings are insignificant in
number, while a great number of small tenants are in search
of land, there the distribution of the large holdings can
prove a sure means of winning the peasantry for the revolution, while the preservation of the large estates can be of
no value for the provisioning of the towns. The first and
most important task of the proletarian state is to secure a
lasting victory. The proletariat must put up with a temporary decline of production so long as it makes for the success
of the revolution. Only by persuading the middle peasantry
to maintain a neutral attitude, and by gaining the support of
a large part, if not the whole, of the small peasantry, can the
lasting maintenance of the proletarian power be secured.

At any rate, where the land of the large owners is being

141

distributed, the interests of the agricultural proletariat must be of primary consideration.

The implements of large estates must be confiscated and converted into state property absolutely intact, but on the unfailing condition that after these implements will have served the interests of the large State farms, they should be put at the disposal of the small peasants gratis, subject to conditions worked out by the proletarian state.

If just at first after the proletarian coup d'état, not only the immediate confiscation of the big estates becomes absolutely necessary, but also the banishment or internment of all landowners as leaders of the counter-revolution and relentless oppressors of the whole rural population, the proletarian state, in proportion to its consolidation not only in the towns but in the country as well, must systematically strive to take advantage of all the forces of this class, of all those who possess valuable experience, learning, organization talent, and must use them (under special control of the most reliable Communist workers) in order to organize large agriculture on Socialist principles.

7. The victory of Socialism over capitalism, the consolidation of socialism, will be definitely secured at the time when the proletarian state power, after having finally subdued all resistance of the exploiters and secured for itself a complete and absolute submission, will reorganize the whole industry· on the basis of wholesale collective production and a new technical condition (founded on the electrification of agriculture). This alone will afford a possibility of such a radical help in the technical and the social sense, accorded by the town to the backward and dispersed country, that this help will create the material base for an enomous increase of the productivity of agricultural and general farming work, and will incite the small farmers by force of example and for

their own benefit to change to large collective machine agriculture.

Most particularly in the rural districts a real possibility of successful struggle for Socialism requires in the first place that all Communist parties educate the industrial proletariat to the consciousness of the necessity of sacrifice on its part, and the readiness to sacrifice itself for the overthrow of the bourgeoisie and the consolidation of the proletarian power is based on the proletariat's knowing how to organize and to lead the working and exploited masses, and on the vanguard's being ready for the greatest sacrifices and for heroism. In the second place a possibility of success requires that the laboring and most exploited masses in the country should experience an immediate and great improvement of their position caused by the victory of the proletariat, and at the expense of the exploiters. Unless this is done, the industrial proletariat cannot depend on the support of the rural districts, and cannot secure the provisionment of the town with food-stuffs.

8. The enormous difficulty of organization and education for the revolutionary struggle of the agrarian laboring masses placed by capitalism in conditions of particular oppression, dispersion and often a mediaeval dependence, require from the Communist parties a special attention to the strike movement in the rural districts. It requires an enforced support and wide development of mass strikes of the agrarian proletarians and semi-proletarians. The experience of the Russian revolutions of 1905 and 1917, confirmed and enlarged now by the experience of Germany, Poland, Italy, England, and other advanced countries shows that only the development of mass strike struggle (under certain conditions the small peasants are also to be drawn into these strikes) will shake the inactivity of the country population,

143

arouse in them a class consciousness and the consciousness of the necessity of class organization in the exploited masses in the country, and show them the obvious practical advantage of their joining the town workers. From this standpoint the promotion of unions of agricultural workers and the co-operation of Communists in the land and lumber workers organizations are of great importance. The Communists must likewise support the co-operative organizations formed by the exploited agricultural population closely connected with the revolutionary labor movement. A vigorous agitation is likewise to be carried on among the small peasants.

The Congress of the Communist International denounces as traitors those Socialists—unfortunately there are such not only in the yellow Second International, but also among the three most important European parties which have left the Second International—who are not only indifferent toward the strike struggle in the rural districts but who oppose it (as does Kautsky) on the ground that it might cause a falling-off of the production of foodstuffs. No program and no solemn declarations have any value if the fact is not in evidence, testified by actual deeds, that the Communists and the labor leaders know how to put above all the development of the proletarian revolution and its victory, and are ready to make the utmost sacrifices for the sake of this victory. Unless this is a fact, there is no issue, no escape from starvation, dissolution and new imperialistic wars.

The Communist parties must make all efforts possible to start as soon as possible setting up Soviets in the country, and these soviets must be chiefly composed of wage-workers and semi-proletarians. Only by being in close connection with the mass strike struggle of the most oppressed class will the Soviets be able to serve fully their ends, and become

144

sufficiently firm to dominate (and later on to include in their ranks) the small peasants. But if the strike struggle is not yet developed, and the ability to organize the agrarian proletariat is weak because of the strong oppression by the landowners and the landed peasants, and also because of the want of support from the industrial workers and their unions, the organization of the Soviets in the rural districts will require a long preparation by means of creating small Communist nuclei, of intensive propaganda expounding in a most popular form the demands of the Communists and illustrating the reasons of these demands by specially convincing cases of exploitation and pressure by systematic excursions of industrial workers into the country, etc.

PART 3

THE PROGRAMME
OF THE COMMUNIST INTERNATIONAL

Adopted by the Sixth World Congress,
September 1, 1928, Moscow

INTRODUCTION

THE EPOCH OF IMPERIALISM is the epoch of moribund capitalism. The world war of 1914-1918 and the general crisis of capitalism to which it led, being the direct result of the sharp contradictions between the growth of productive forces of world economy and the national State barriers which intersect it, have shown and proved that the material prerequisites for Socialism have already ripened in the womb of capitalist society, that the shell of capitalism has become an intolerable hindrance to the further development of mankind and that history has brought to the forefront the task of the revolutionary overthrow of the yoke of capitalism.

Imperialism subjects large masses of the proletariat of all countries—from the centers of capitalist might to the most remote corners of the colonial world—to the dictatorship of the finance-capitalist plutocracy. With elemental force, imperialism exposes and accentuates all the contradictions of capitalist society; it carries class oppression to the utmost limits, intensifies the struggle between capitalist governments, inevitably gives rise to world-wide imperialist wars that shake the whole prevailing system of relationships to their foundations and inexorably lead to the World Proletarian Revolution.

Binding the whole world in chains of finance capital; forcing its yoke upon the proletariat and the nations and races of all countries by methods of blood, iron and starvation; sharpening to an immeasurable degree the exploitation, oppression and enslavement of the proletariat and confronting it with the immediate task of conquering the power—

149

imperialism creates the necessity for closely uniting the workers of all countries, irrespective of State frontiers, and of differences of nationality, culture, language, race, sex or profession in a single international army of the proletariat. Thus, while imperialism develops and completes the process of creating the material prerequisites for Socialism, it at the same time musters the army of its own grave-diggers and compels the proletariat to organize in a militant international workers' association.

On the other hand, imperialism splits off the best-provided-for section of the working class from the main mass of the workers. Bribed and corrupted by imperialism, this upper stratum of the working class constitutes the leading element in the Social-Democratic parties; it is interested in the imperialist plunder of the colonies, is loyal to its own bourgeoisie and "its own" imperialist State, and, in the midst of decisive battles, fought on the side of the class enemy of the proletariat. The split that occurred in the Socialist movement in 1914 as a result of this treachery, and the subsequent treachery of the Social-Democratic parties—which in reality have become bourgeois labor parties, demonstrated that the international proletariat will be able to fulfill its historical mission—to throw off the yoke of imperialism and establish the proletarian dictatorship—only by ruthless struggle against Social Democracy. Hence, the organization of the forces of the international revolution becomes possible only on the platform of Communism. In opposition to the opportunistic Second International of Social-Democracy—which has become the agency of imperialism in the ranks of the working class—inevitably rises the Third, Communist International, the international organization of the working class, the embodiment of real unity of the revolutionary workers of the whole world.

The war of 1914-1918 gave rise to the first attempts to establish a new, revolutionary International, as a counterpoise to the Second, Social-Chauvinist International, and as a weapon of resistance to bellicose imperialism. (Zimmerwald, Kienthal.) The victorious proletarian revolution in Russia gave an impetus to the formation of Communist Parties in the centers of capitalism and in the colonies. In 1919, the Communist International was formed, and for the first time in world history the most advanced strata of the European and American proletariat were really united in the process of practical revolutionary struggle with the proletariat of China and India and with the colored toilers of Africa and America.

As the united and centralized international Party of the proletariat, the Communist International is the only Party to continue the principles of the First International, and to carry them out upon the new mass foundation of the revolutionary proletarian movement. The experience gathered from the first imperialist war, from the subsequent period of revolutionary crises of capitalism, from the series of revolutions in Europe and in the colonial countries; the experience gathered from the dictatorship of the proletariat and the building up of Socialism in the U.S.S.R. and from the work of all the Sections of the Communist International as recorded in the decisions of its Congresses; finally, the fact that the struggle between the imperialist bourgeoisie and the proletariat is more and more assuming an international character—all this creates the need for a uniform program of the Communist International that shall be common for all Sections of the Communist International. This program of the Communist International, being the supreme critical generalization of the whole body of historical experience of the international revolutionary proletarian movement, becomes the program of struggle for the World Proletarian Dictatorship, the program of struggle for World Communism.

Uniting, as it does, the revolutionary workers, who lead the millions of oppressed and exploited against the bourgeoisie and its "socialist" agents, the Communist International regards itself as the historical successor to the "Communist League" and the First International led by Marx, and as the inheritor of the best of the pre-war traditions of the Second International. The First International laid the ideological foundation for the international proletarian struggle for Socialism. The Second International, in the best period of its existence, prepared the ground for the expansion of the labor movement among the masses. The Third, Communist International, in continuing the work of the First International, and in accepting the fruits of the work of the Second International, resolutely lopped off the latter's opportunism, social chauvinism, and bourgeois distortion of Socialism and set out to realize the dictatorship of the proletariat. In this manner the Communist International continues the glorious and heroic traditions of the international labor movement; of the English Chartists and the French insurrectionists of 1831; of the French and German working class revolutionaries of 1848; of the immortal warriors and martyrs of the Paris Commune; of the valiant soldiers of the German, Hungarian and Finnish revolutions; of the workers under former tsarist despotism—the victorious bearers of the proletarian dictatorship; of the Chinese proletarians—the heroes of Canton and Shanghai.

Basing itself on the experience of the revolutionary labor movement on all Continents and of all peoples, the Communist International, in its theoretical and practical work, stands wholly and unreservedly upon the ground of revolutionary Marxism, and its further development, Leninism, which is nothing else but Marxism of the epoch of imperialism and proletarian revolution.

Advocating and propagating the dialectical Materialism of Marx and Engels and employing it as a revolutionary method of conceiving reality, with the view to the revolutionary transformation of this reality, the Communist International wages an active struggle against all forms of bourgeois philosophy and against all forms of theoretical and practical opportunism. Standing on the ground of consistent proletarian class struggle and subordinating the temporary, partial, group and national interests of the proletariat to its lasting, general, international interests, the Communist International mercilessly exposes all forms of the doctrine of "class peace" that the reformists have accepted from the bourgeoise. Expressing the historical need for an international organization of revolutionary proletarians—the grave-diggers of the capitalist order—the Communist International is the only international force that has for its program the dictatorship of the proletariat and Communism, and that openly comes out as the organizer of the International Proletarian Revolution.

I

THE WORLD SYSTEM OF CAPITALISM
ITS DEVELOPMENT
AND INEVITABLE DOWNFALL

1. *The Dynamic Laws of Capitalism and the Epoch of Industrial Capital*

THE CHARACTERISTIC FEATURES of capitalist society which arose on the basis of commodity production are monopoly of the most important and vital means of production by the capitalist class and big landlords; the exploitation of the wage labor of the proletariat, which, being deprived of the means of production, is compelled to sell its labor power; the production of commodities for profit and, linked up with all this, the planless and anarchic character of the process of production as a whole. Exploitation relationships and the economic domination of the bourgeoise find their political expression in the organized capitalist State, the instrument for the suppression of the proletariat.

The history of capitalism has entirely confirmed the theories of Marx and Engels concerning the laws of development of capitalist society and concerning the contradictions of this development that must inevitably lead to the downfall of the whole capitalist system.

In its quest for profits the bourgeoisie was compelled to develop the productive forces on an ever-increasing scale and to strengthen and expand the domination of capitalist relationships of production. Thus, the development of

154

capitalism constantly reproduces on a wider scale all the inherent contradictions of the capitalist system, primarily, the vital contradiction between the social character of labor and private acquisition, between the growth of the productive forces and the property relations of capitalism. The predominance of private property in the means of production and the anarchy prevailing in the process of production have disturbed the equilibrium between the various branches of production; for a growing contradiction developed between the tendency towards unlimited expansion of production and the restricted consumption of the masses of the proletariat (general over-production), and this resulted in periodical devastating crises and mass unemployment among the proletariat. The predominance of private property also found expression in the competition that prevailed in each separate capitalist country as well as on the constantly expanding world market. This latter form of capitalist rivalry resulted in a number of wars, which are the inevitable accompaniment of capitalist development.

On the other hand, the technical and economic advantages of mass production have resulted in the squeezing out and destruction in the competitive struggle of the pre-capitalist economic forms and to the ever-increasing concentration and centralization of capital. In the sphere of industry this law of concentration and centralization of capital manifested itself primarily in the direct ruin of small enterprises and partly in their being reduced to the position of auxiliary units of large enterprises. In the domain of agriculture which, owing to the existence of the monopoly in land and absolute rent, must inevitably lag behind the general rate of development, this law not only found expression in the process of differentiation that took place among the peasantry and in the proletarianization of broad strata of the latter, but also and mainly in the open and concealed subordination of small peasant economy to the domination of big capital; small farming has been able to maintain a nominal independence only at the price of extreme intensification of labor and systematic under-consumption.

The ever-growing application of machinery, the constant improvements in technics and, consequently, the uninter-rupted rise in the organic composition of capital, accom-panied by still further division, increased productivity and intensity of labor, and meant also increased employment of female and child labor, the formation of enormous indus-trial reserve armies which are constantly replenished by the proletarianized peasantry who are forced to leave their villages as well as by the ruined small and middle urban bourgeoisie. The collection of a handful of capitalist mag-nates at one pole of social relationships and of a gigantic mass of the proletariat at the other; the constantly increas-ing rate of exploitation of the working class, the reproduc-tion on a wider scale of the deepest contradictions of capi-talism and their consequences (crises, wars, etc.); the con-stant growth of social inequality, the rising discontent of the proletariat united and schooled by the mechanism of capitalist production itself—all this has inevitably under-mined the foundations of capitalism and has brought nearer the day of its collapse.

Simultaneously, a profound change has taken place in the social and cultural life of capitalist society; the parasitical decadence of the rentier group of the bourgeoisie; the break up of the family, which expresses the growing contradiction between the mass participation of women in social produc-tion and the forms of family and domestic life largely in-herited from previous economic epochs; the growing shal-

156

lowness and degeneracy of cultural and ideological life resulting from the minute specialization of labor, the monstrous forms of urban life and the restrictedness of rural life; the incapability of the bourgeoisie, notwithstanding the enormous achievements of the natural sciences, to create a synthetically scientific philosophy, and the growth of ideological, mystical and religious superstition, are all phenomena signalizing the approach of the historical end of the capitalist system.

2. The Era of Finance Capital (Imperialism)

The period of industrial capitalism was, in the main, a period of "free competition"; a period of a steady development and expansion of capitalism throughout the whole world, when the as yet unoccupied colonies were being divided up and conquered by armed force; a period of continuous growth of the inherent contradictions of capitalism, the burden of which fell mainly upon the systematically plundered, crushed and oppressed colonial periphery.

Towards the beginning of the twentieth century, this period was replaced by the period of imperialism, during which capitalism developed spasmodically and conflictingly; free competition rapidly gave way to monopoly, the previously "available" colonial lands were all divided up, and the struggle for a redistribution of colonies and spheres of influence inevitably began to assume primarily the form of a struggle by force of arms.

Thus, the entire scope and truly world wide scale of the contradictions of capitalism become most glaringly revealed

157

in the epoch of imperialism (finance capitalism), which, from the historical standpoint, signifies a new form of capitalism, a new system of relationships between the various parts of world capitalist economy and a change in the relationship between the principal classes of capitalist society.

This new historical period set in as a result of the operation of the principal dynamic laws of capitalist society. It grew out of the development of industrial capitalism, and is the historical continuation of the latter. It sharpened the manifestations of all the fundamental tendencies and dynamic laws of capitalist development, of all its fundamental contradictions and antagonisms. The law of the concentration and centralization of capital led to the formation of powerful combines (cartels, syndicates, trusts), to new forms of gigantic combinations of enterprises, linked up into one system by the banks. The merging of industrial capital with bank capital, the absorption of big land ownership into the general system of capitalist organization, and the monopolistic character of this form of capitalism transformed the epoch of industrial capital into the epoch of finance capital. "Free competition" of the period of industrial capitalism, which replaced feudal monopoly and the monopoly of merchant capital, became itself transformed into finance capital monopoly. At the same time, although capitalistic organizations grow out of free competition, they do not eliminate competition, but exist side by side and hover over it, and thus give rise to a series of exceptionally great and acute contradictions, frictions and conflicts.

The growing application of complex machinery, of chemical processes and of electrical energy; the resulting higher organic composition of capital, and consequently, decline in the rate of profit, which only the biggest monopolist combines are able to counteract for a time by their policy of high cartel prices, still further stimulate the quest for colonial super-profits and the struggle for a new division of the world. Standardized mass production creates the demand for new foreign markets. The growing demand for raw materials and fuel intensifies the race for their sources. Lastly, the system of high protection, which hinders the export of merchandise and secures additional profit for exported capital, creates additional stimuli for the export of capital. Export of capital becomes, therefore, the decisive and specific form of economic contact between the various parts of world capitalist economy. The total effect of all this is that the monopolist ownership of colonial markets, of sources of raw materials and of spheres of investment of capital extremely accentuates the general unevenness of capitalist development and sharpens the conflicts between the "great powers" of finance capital over the redistribution of the colonies and spheres of influence.

The growth of the productive forces of world economy thus leads to the further internationalization of economic life and simultaneously leads to a struggle for redistribution of the world, already divided up among the biggest finance-capital States, to a change in and sharpening of the forms of this struggle and to the method of forcing down prices being superseded to an increasing degree by the method of forcible pressure (boycott, high protection, tariff wars, wars proper, etc.). Consequently, the monopolistic form of capitalism is inevitably accompanied by imperialist wars, which, by the area they embrace and the destructiveness of their technique, have no parallel in world history.

3. The Forces of Imperialism and the Forces of Revolution

Expressing the tendency to the unification of the various sections of the dominant class, the imperialist form of capitalism places the broad masses of the proletariat in opposition, not to a single employer, but, to an increasing degree, to the capitalist class as a whole and to the capitalist State. On the other hand, this form of capitalism breaks down the national barriers that have become too restricted for it, widens the scope of the capitalist State power of the dominant Great Power and brings it in opposition to vast masses of nationally oppressed peoples in the so-called small nations as well as in the colonies. Finally, this form of capitalism brings the imperialist States most sharply in opposition to each other.

This being the case, State power, which is becoming the dictatorship of the finance-capitalist oligarchy and the expression of its concentrated might, acquires special significance for the bourgeoise. The functions of this multinational imperialist State grow in all directions. The development of State capitalist forms, which facilitate the struggle in foreign markets (mobilization of industry for war purposes) as well as the struggle against the working class; the monstrous growth of militarism (armies, naval and air fleets, the employment of chemistry and bacteriology); the increasing pressure of the imperialist State upon the working class (the growth of exploitation and direct suppression of the workers on the one hand and the systematic policy of bribing the bureaucratic reformist leadership on the other), all this expresses the enormous growth in the power of the State. Under these circumstances, every more or less important action of the proletariat becomes transformed

160

into an action against the State power, i.e., into political action.

Hence the development of capitalism, and particularly the imperialist epoch of its development, reproduces the fundamental contradictions of capitalism on an increasingly magnified scale. Competition among small capitalists ceases only to make way for competition among big capitalists; where competition among big capitalists subsides, it flares up between gigantic combinations of capitalist magnates and their governments; local and national crises become transformed into crises affecting a number of countries and, subsequently, into world crises; local wars give way to wars between coalitions of States and to world wars; the class struggle changes from isolated actions of single groups of workers into nation-wide conflicts and, subsequently, into an international struggle of the world proletariat against the world bourgeoisie. Finally, two main revolutionary forces are organizing against the organized might of finance capital;—on the one hand the workers in the capitalist States, on the other hand, the victims of the oppression of foreign capital, the masses of the people in the colonies, marching under the leadership and the hegemony of the international revolutionary proletarian movement.

However, this fundamental revolutionary tendency is temporarily paralyzed by the fact that certain sections of the European, North American and Japanese proletariat are bribed by the imperialist bourgeoisie, and by the treachery of the national bourgeoisie in the semi-colonial and colonial countries who are scared by the revolutionary mass movement. The bourgeoisie in imperialist countries—which is able to secure additional surplus profits from the position it holds in the world market (more developed techniques, export of capital to countries with a higher rate of profit, etc.), and form the proceeds of its plunder of the colonies and semi-colonies—was able to raise the wages of its "own" workers out of these surplus profits, thus giving these workers an interest in the development of "home" capitalism, in the plunder of the colonies and in being loyal to the imperialist States. This systematic bribery was and is being very widely practiced in the most powerful imperialist countries and finds most striking expression in the ideology and practice of the labor aristocracy and the bureaucratic strata of the working class, i.e., the Social-Democratic and trade union leaders, who proved to be the direct agencies of bourgeois influence among the proletariat and stalwart pillars of the capitalist system.

By stimulating the growth of the corrupt upper stratum of the working class, however, imperialism, in the end, destroys its influence upon the working class, because the growing contradictions of imperialism, the worsening of the conditions of the broad masses of the workers, the mass unemployment among the proletariat, the enormous cost of military conflicts and the burdens they entail, the fact that certain Powers have lost their monopolistic position in the world market, the break-away of the colonies, etc., serve to undermine the basis of Social Democracy among the masses. Similarly, the systematic bribery of the various sections of the bourgeoisie in the colonies and semi-colonies, their betrayal of the national-revolutionary movement and their rapprochement with the imperialist powers can paralyze the development of the revolutionary crisis only for a time. In the final analysis, this leads to the intensification of imperialist oppression, to the decline of the influence of the national bourgeoisie upon the masses of the people, to the sharpening of the revolutionary crisis, to the unleashing of the agrarian revolution of the broad masses of the peasantry and to the creation of conditions favorable for the establishment of the hegemony of the proletariat in the colonies and dependencies in the popular mass struggle for independence and complete national liberation.

4. *Imperialism and the Downfall of Capitalism*

Imperialism has greatly developed the productive forces of world capitalism. It has completed the preparation of all the material prerequisites for the Socialist organization of society. By its wars it has demonstrated that the productive forces of world economy, which have outgrown the restricted boundaries of imperialist States, demand the organization of economy on a world, or international scale. Imperialism tries to remove this contradiction by hacking a road with fire and sword towards a single world State-capitalist trust, which is to organize the whole of world economy. This sanguinary utopia is being extolled by the Social-Democratic ideologists as the peaceful method of newly "organized" capitalism. In reality, this utopia encounters insurmountable objective obstacles of such magnitude that capitalism must inevitably fall beneath the weight of its own contradictions. The law of uneven development of capitalism, which becomes intensified in the epoch of imperialism, renders firm and durable international combinations of imperialist power impossible. On the other hand, imperialist wars, which are developing into world wars, and by which the law of the centralization of capitalism strives to reach its world limit—a single world trust—are accompanied by so much destruction and place such burdens upon the shoulders of the working class and of the millions of colonial proletarians and peasants, that capitalism must inevitably perish beneath the blows of the proletarian revolution long before this goal is reached.

Being the highest phase of capitalist development, developing the productive forces of world economy to enormous dimensions, refashioning the whole world after its own image, imperialism draws within the orbit of finance-capitalist exploitation all colonies, all races and all nations. At the same time, however, the monopolistic form of capital increasingly develops the elements of parasitical degeneration, decay and decline of capitalism. By destroying, to some extent, the driving force of competition, by conducting a policy of cartel prices, and by having undivided mastery of the market, monopoly capital reveals a tendency to retard the further development of the forces of production. In squeezing enormous sums of surplus profits out of the millions of colonial workers and peasants and in accumulating colossal incomes from this exploitation, Imperialism is creating a type of decaying and parasitically degenerate rentier-class, as well as whole strata of parasites who live by clipping coupons. While completing the process of creating the material pre-requisites for Socialism (the concentration of means of production, the enormous socialization of labor, the growth of labor organizations), the epoch of imperialism at the same time intensifies the antagonisms among the "Great Powers" and gives rise to wars which cause the break-up of single world economy. Imperialism is therefore moribund and decaying capitalism. It is the final stage of development of the capitalist system. It is the threshold of world social revolution.

Hence, international proletarian revolution logically emerges out of the conditions of development of capitalism

164

generally, and out of its imperialist phase in particular. The capitalist system as a whole is approaching its final collapse. The dictatorship of finance capital is perishing, to give way to the dictatorship of the Proletariat.

THE GENERAL CRISIS OF CAPITALISM
AND THE FIRST PHASE
OF WORLD REVOLUTION

1. *The World War*
and the Progress of the Revolutionary Crisis

THE IMPERIALIST STRUGGLE among the largest capitalist States for the redistribution of the globe led to the first Imperialist World War (1914-1918). This war shook the whole system of world capitalism and marked the beginning of the period of its general crisis. It bent to its service the entire national economy of the belligerent countries, thus creating the mailed fist of State capitalism; it increased unproductive expenditures to enormous dimensions, destroyed enormous quantities of means of production and human labor power, ruined large masses of the population and imposed incalculable burdens upon the industrial workers, the peasants and the colonial peoples. It inevitably led to the intensification of the class struggle, which grew into open, revolutionary mass action and civil war. The imperialist front was broken at its weakest link, in tsarist Russia. The February Revolution of 1917 overthrew the domination of the autocracy of the big landowning class. The October Revolution overthrew the rule of the bourgeoisie. This victorious proletarian revolution expropriated the expropriators, took the means of production from the landlords and the capitalists, and for the first time in human history, set up and consolidated the dictatorship of the proletariat in an

enormous country, brought into being a new, Soviet type of
State and laid the foundations for the international proletarian revolution.

The powerful shock to which the whole of world capitalism was subjected, the sharpening of the class struggle
and the direct influence of the October proletarian Revolution gave rise to a series of revolutions and revolutionary
actions on the Continent of Europe as well as in the colonial and semi-colonial countries: January, 1918, the proletarian revolution in Finland; August, 1918, the so-called
"rice riots" in Japan; November, 1918, the revolutions in
Austria and Germany, which overthrew the semi-feudal
monarchist régime; March, 1919, the proletarian revolution in Hungary and the uprising in Korea; April, 1919, the
Soviet Government in Bavaria; January, 1920, the bourgeois-
national revolution in Turkey; September, 1920, the seizure
of the factories by the workers in Italy; March, 1921, the
rising of the advanced workers of Germany; September,
1923, the uprising in Bulgaria; Autumn, 1923, the revolutionary crisis in Germany; December, 1924, the uprising in
Estonia; April, 1925, the uprising in Morocco; August, 1925,
uprising in Syria; May, 1926, the general strike in England;
July, 1927, the proletarian uprising in Vienna. These events,
as well as events like the uprising in Indonesia, the deep ferment in India, the great Chinese revolution, which shook
the whole Asiatic Continent, are links in one and the same
international revolutionary chain, constituent parts of the
profound general crisis of capitalism. This international
revolutionary process embraced the immediate struggle for
the dictatorship of the proletariat, as well as national wars
of liberation and colonial uprisings against imperialism,
which inseparably go together with the agrarian mass movement of millions of peasants. Thus, an enormous mass of

humanity was swept into the revolutionary torrent. World history entered a new phase of development—a phase of prolonged general crisis of the capitalist system. In this process, the unity of world economy found expression in the international character of the revolution, while the uneven development of its separate parts was expressed in the absence of simultaneity in the outbreak of revolution in the different countries.

The first attempts at revolutionary overthrow, which sprang from the acute crisis of capitalism (1918-1921) ended in the victory and consolidation of the dictatorship of the proletariat in the U.S.S.R. and in the defeat of the proletariat in a number of other countries. These defeats were primarily due to the treacherous tactics of the Social Democratic and reformist trade union leaders, but they were also due to the fact that the majority of the working class had not yet accepted the lead of the Communists and that in a number of important countries Communist Parties had not yet been established at all. As a result of these defeats, which created the opportunity for intensifying the exploitation of the mass of the proletariat and the colonial peoples and for severely depressing their standard of living, the bourgeoisie was able to achieve a partial stabilization of capitalist relations.

2. The Revolutionary Crisis
and Counter-Revolutionary Social Democracy

During the progress of the international revolution, the leading cadres of the Social-Democratic parties and of the reformist trade unions on the one hand, and the militant capitalist organizations of the Fascist type on the other, acquired special significance as a powerful counter-revolutionary force actively fighting against the revolution and actively supporting the partial stabilization of capitalism.

The war crisis of 1914-1918 was accompanied by the disgraceful collapse of the Social-Democratic Second International. Acting in complete violation of the thesis of the "Communist Manifesto" written by Marx-Engels, that the proletariat has no fatherland under capitalism and, in complete violation of the anti-war resolutions passed by the Stuttgart and Basel Congresses, the leaders of the Social Democratic parties in the various countries, with a few exceptions, voted for the war credits, came out definitely in defense of the imperialist "fatherland" (i.e., the State organization of the imperialist bourgeoisie) and instead of combatting the imperialist war, became its loyal soldiers, bards and propagandists (social-patriotism, which grew into social-imperialism). In the subsequent period, Social Democracy supported the predatory treaties (Brest-Litovsk, Versailles); it actively aligned itself with the militarists in the bloody suppression of proletarian uprisings (Noske); it conducted armed warfare against the first proletarian republic (Soviet Russia); it despicably betrayed the victorious proletariat (Hungary); it joined the imperialist League of Nations (Albert Thomas, Paul Boncour, Vandervelde); it openly supported the imperialist slave-owners against the colonial slaves (the British Labor Party); it actively supported the most reactionary executioners of the working class (Bulgaria, Poland); it took upon itself the initiative in securing the passage of imperialist "military laws" (France); it betrayed the general strike of the British proletariat; it helped and is still helping to strangle China and India (the MacDonald Government); it acts as the propagandist for the imperialist League of Nations; it is capital's herald and organizer of the struggle against the dictatorship of the proletariat in the U.S.S.R. (Kautsky, Hilferding).

In its systematic conduct of this counter-revolutionary policy, Social Democracy operates on two flanks: the right wing of Social Democracy, avowedly counter-revolutionary, is essential for negotiating and maintaining direct contact with the bourgeoisie; the left wing is essential for the subtle deception of the workers. While playing with pacifist and at times even with revolutionary phrases, "Left wing" Social Democracy, in practice, acts against the workers, particularly in acute and critical situations (the British "Independents" and the "Left" leaders of the General Council during the General Strike in 1926; Otto Bauer and Co., at the time of the Vienna uprising), and is therefore, the most dangerous faction in the Social Democratic parties. While serving the interests of the bourgeoisie in the working class and being wholly in favor of class cooperation and coalition with the bourgeoisie, Social Democracy, at certain periods, is compelled to play the part of an opposition party and even to pretend that it is defending the class interests of the proletariat in its industrial struggle, in order thereby to win the confidence of a section of the working class and to be in a position more shamefully to betray the lasting interests of the working class, particularly in the midst of decisive class battles.

The principal function of Social Democracy at the present time is to disrupt the essential militant unity of the proletariat in its struggle against imperialism. In splitting and disrupting the united front of the proletarian struggle against capital, Social Democracy serves as the mainstay of imperialism in the working class. International Social Democracy of all shades; the Second International and its trade union branch, the Amsterdam Federation of Trade Unions, have become the last reserve of bourgeois society and its most reliable pillar of support.

3. The Crisis of Capitalism and Fascism

Side by side with Social Democracy, with whose aid the bourgeoisie suppresses the workers or lulls their class vigilance, stands Fascism.

The epoch of imperialism, the sharpening of the class struggle and the growth of elements of civil war—particularly after the imperialist war—led to the bankruptcy of parliamentarism. Hence, the adoption of "new" methods and forms of administration (for example the system of inner cabinets, the formation of oligarchical groups acting behind the scenes, the deterioration and falsification of the function of "popular representation," the restriction and annulment of "democratic liberties," etc.). Under certain special historical conditions, the progress of this bourgeois, imperialist, reactionary offensive assumes the form of Fascism. These conditions are: instability of capitalist relationships; the existence of considerable declassed social elements, the pauperization of broad strata of the urban petty-bourgeoisie and of the intelligentsia; discontent among the rural petty-bourgeoisie and, finally, the constant menace of mass proletarian action. In order to stabilize and perpetuate its rule, the bourgeoisie is compelled to an increasing degree to abandon the parliamentary system in favor of the Fascist system, which is independent of inter-Party arrangements, and combinations. The Fascist system is a system of direct dictatorship, ideologically masked by the "national idea" and

171

representation of the "professions" (in reality, representation of the various groups of the ruling class). It is a system that resorts to a peculiar form of social demagogy (anti-semitism, occasional sorties against usuers' capital and gestures of impatience with the parliamentary "talking shop") in order to utilize the discontent of the petty-bourgeois, the intellectual and other strata of society, and to corruption —the creation of a compact and well paid hierarchy of Fascist units, a party apparatus and a bureaucracy. At the same time, Fascism strives to permeate the working class by recruiting the most backward strata of the workers to its ranks, by playing upon their discontent, by taking advantage of the inaction of Social Democracy, etc. The principal aim of Fascism is to destroy the revolutionary labor vanguard, i.e., the Communist Sections and leading units of the proletariat. The combination of social democracy, corruption and active white terror, in conjunction with extreme imperialist aggression in the sphere of foreign politics, are the characteristic features of Fascism. In periods of acute crisis for the bourgeoisie, Fascism resorts to anti-capitalist phraseology, but, after it has established itself at the helm of State, it casts aside its anti-capitalist rattle and discloses itself as a terrorist dictatorship of big capital.

The bourgeoisie resorts either to the method of Fascism or to the method of coalition with Social Democracy according to the changes in the political situation; while Social Democracy itself often plays a Fascist role in periods when the situation is critical for capitalism.

In the process of development Social Democracy reveals Fascist tendencies which, however, does not prevent it, in other political situations, from acting as a sort of Fronde against the bourgeois government in the capacity of an opposition party. The Fascist method and the method of

172

coalition with Social-Democracy, are not the methods usually employed in "normal" capitalist conditions; they are symptoms of the general capitalist crisis, and are employed by the bourgeoisie in order to stem the advance of the revolution.

4. The Contradictions of Capitalist Stabilization
and the Inevitability
of the Revolutionary Collapse of Capitalism

Experience throughout the post-war historical period has shown that the stabilization achieved by the repression of the working class and the systematic depression of its standard of living can be only a partial, transient and decaying stabilization.

The spasmodic and feverish development of technics, bordering in some countries on a new technical revolution, the accelerated process of concentration and centralization of capital, the formation of giant trusts and of "national" and "international" monopolies, the merging of trusts with the State power and the growth of world capitalist economy cannot, however, eliminate the general crisis of the capitalist system. The breakup of world economy into a capitalist and a socialist sector, the shrinking of markets and the anti-imperialist movement in the colonies intensify all the contradictions of capitalism, which is developing on a new, post-war basis. This very technical progress and rationalization of industry, the reverse side of which is the closing down and liquidation of numerous enterprises, the restriction of production, and the ruthless and destructive exploi-

173

tation of labor power, leads to chronic unemployment on a scale never before experienced. The absolute deterioration of the conditions of the working class becomes a fact even in certain highly developed capitalist countries. The growing competition between imperialist countries, the constant menace of war and the growing intensity of class conflicts prepare the ground for a new and higher stage of development of the general crisis of capitalism and of the world proletarian revolution.

As a result of the first round of imperialist wars (the world war of 1914-1918) and of the October victory of the working class in the former Russian tsarist Empire, world economy has been split into two fundamentally hostile camps: the camp of the imperialist states and the camp of the dictatorship of the Proletariat in the U.S.S.R. The difference in class structure and in the class character of the government in the two camps, the fundamental differences in the aims each pursues in internal, foreign, economic and cultural policy, the fundamentally different courses of their development, brings the capitalist world into sharp conflict with the victorious proletarian State. Within the framework of a formerly uniform world economy, two antagonistic systems are now contesting against each other: the system of Capitalism and the system of Socialism. The class struggle, which hitherto was conducted in circumstances when the proletariat was not in possession of State power, is now being conducted on an enormous and really world scale; the working class of the world has now its own State—the one and only fatherland of the international proletariat. The existence of the Soviet Union and the influence it exercises upon the toiling and oppressed masses all over the world is in itself a most striking expression of the profound crisis of the world capitalist system and of the expansion and intensi-

174

fication of the class struggle to a degree hitherto without parallel in history.

The capitalist world, powerless to eliminate its inherent contradictions, strives to establish international associations (the League of Nations) the main purpose of which is to retard the irresistible growth of the revolutionary crisis and to strangle the Soviet Proletarian Republics by war or blockade. At the same time, all the forces of the revolutionary proletariat and of the oppressed colonial masses are rallying around the U.S.S.R. The world coalition of capital, unstable, internally corroded, but armed to the teeth, is confronted by a single world coalition of Labor. Thus, as a result of the first round of imperialist wars a new, fundamental antagonism has arisen of world historical scope and significance: the antagonism between the U.S.S.R. and the capitalist world.

Meanwhile, the inherent antagonisms within the capitalist sector of world economy itself have become intensified. The shifting of the economic center of the world to the United States of America and the fact of the "Dollar Republic" having become a world exploiter have caused the relations between United States and European capitalism, primarily British capitalism, to become strained. The conflict between Great Britain—the most powerful of the old, conservative imperialist States—and the United States—the greatest of the young imperialist States, which has already won world hegemony for itself, is becoming the pivot of the world conflicts among the finance capitalist States. Germany, though plundered by the Versailles Peace, is now economically recovered; she is resuming the path of imperialist politics, and once again she stands out as a serious competitor on the world market. The Pacific is becoming involved in a tangle of contradictions which center

175

mainly around the antagonism between America and Japan. Simultaneously, the antagonism of interests among the unstable and constantly changing groupings of powers is increasing, while the minor powers serve as the auxiliary instruments in the hands of the imperialist giants and their coalitions.

The growth of the productive capacity of the industrial apparatus of world capitalism, at a time when the European home markets have shrunk as a result of the war, as the result of the Soviet Union dropping out of the system of purely capitalist intercourse and of the close monopoly of the most important sources of raw material and fuel, leads to ever-widening conflicts between the capitalist States. The "peaceful" struggle for oil, rubber, cotton, coal and metals and for a redistribution of markets and spheres for the export of capital is inexorably leading to another world war, the destructiveness of which will increase in proportion to the progress achieved in the furiously developing technique of war.

Simultaneously, the antagonisms between the imperialist home countries and the colonial and semi-colonial countries are growing. The relative weakening of European imperialism as a result of the war, of the development of capitalism in the colonies, of the influence of the Soviet Revolution and of the centrifugal tendencies revealed in the premier maritime and colonial Empire—Great Britain (Canada, Australia, South Africa) has helped to stimulate the movement of rebellion in the colonies and semi-colonies. The great Chinese Revolution, which roused hundreds of millions of the Chinese people to action, caused an enormous breach in the imperialist system. The unceasing revolutionary ferment among hundreds of millions of Indian workers and peasants is threatening to break the domination of the

176

world citadel of imperialism, Great Britain. The growth of tendencies directed against the powerful imperialism of the United States in the Latin-American countries threatens to undermine the expansion of North American capital. Thus, the revolutionary process in the colonies, which is drawing into the struggle against imperialism the overwhelming majority of the world's population that is subjected to the rule of the finance-capitalist oligarchy of a few "Great Powers" of imperialism, also expresses the profound general crisis of capitalism. Even in Europe itself, where imperialism has put a number of small nations under its heel, the national question is a factor that intensifies the inherent contradictions of capitalism.

Finally, the revolutionary crisis is inexorably maturing in the very centers of imperialism: the capitalist offensive against the working class, the attack upon the workers' standard of living, upon their organizations, and their political rights, and the growth of white terror, rouse increasing resistance on the part of the broad masses of the proletariat and intensify the class struggle between the working class and trustified capital. The great battles fought between labor and capital, the accelerated swing to the Left of the masses, the growth in the influence and authority of the Communist Parties; the enormous growth of sympathy of the broad masses of workers for the land of the proletarian dictatorship—all this is a clear symptom of the rise of a new revolutionary tide in the centers of imperialism.

Thus, the system of world imperialism, and with it the partial stabilization of capitalism, is being corroded from various causes: First, the antagonisms and conflicts between the imperialist States; second, the rising for the struggle of vast masses in the colonial countries; third, the action of the revolutionary proletariat in the imperialist home countries;

and lastly, the hegemony exercised over the whole world revolutionary movement by the proletarian dictatorship in the U.S.S.R. The International Revolution is developing.

Against this revolution, imperialism is gathering its forces. Expeditions against the colonies, a new world war, a campaign against the U.S.S.R., are matters which now figure prominently in the politics of imperialism. This must lead to the release of all forces of international revolution and to the inevitable doom of capitalism.

III

THE ULTIMATE AIM
OF THE COMMUNIST INTERNATIONAL—
WORLD COMMUNISM

THE ULTIMATE AIM of the Communist International is to replace world capitalist economy by a world system of Communism. Communist society, the basis for which has been prepared by the whole course of historical development, is mankind's only way out, for it alone can abolish the contradictions of the capitalist system which threaten to degrade and destroy the human race.

Communist society will abolish the class division of society, i.e., simultaneously with the abolition of anarchy in production, it will abolish all forces of exploitation and oppression of man by man. Society will no longer consist of antagonistic classes in conflict with each other, but will represent a united commonwealth of labor. For the first time in its history mankind will take its fate into its own hands. Instead of destroying innumerable human lives and incalculable wealth in struggles between classes and nations, mankind will devote all its energy to the struggle against the forces of nature, to the development and strengthening of its own collective might.

After abolishing private ownership in the means of production and converting them into social property, the world system of Communism will replace the elemental forces of the world market, of competition and the blind process of social production, by consciously organized and planned production for the purpose of satisfying rapidly growing social needs. With the abolition of competition and anarchy in production, devastating crises and still more devastating wars will disappear. Instead of colossal waste of productive forces and spasmodic development of society—there will be planned utilization of all material resources and painless economic development on the basis of unrestricted, smooth and rapid development of productive forces.

The abolition of private property and the disappearance of classes will do away with the exploitation of man by man. Work will cease to be toiling for the benefit of a class enemy: instead of being merely a means of livelihood it will become a necessity of life: want and economic inequality, the misery of enslaved classes, and a wretched standard of life generally will disappear; the hierarchy created in the division of labor system will be abolished together with the antagonism between mental and manual labor; and the last vestige of the social inequality of sexes will be removed. At the same time, the organs of class domination, and the State in the first place, will disappear also. The State, being the embodiment of class domination, will die out insofar as classes die out, and with it all measures of coercion will expire.

With the disappearance of classes the monopoly of education in every form will be abolished. Culture will become the acquirement of all and the class ideologies of the past will give place to scientific materialist philosophy. Under such circumstances, the domination of man over man, in any form, becomes impossible, and a great field will be opened for the social selection and the harmonious development of all the talents inherent in humanity.

In Communist society no social restrictions will be imposed upon the growth of the forces of production. Private ownership in the means of production, the selfish lust for profits, the artificial retention of the masses in a state of

ignorance, poverty—which retards technical progress in capitalist society, and unproductive expenditures will have no
place in a Communist society. The most expedient utilization of the forces of nature and of the natural conditions of
production in the various parts of the world; the removal
of the antagonism between town and country, that under
capitalism results from the low technical level of agriculture
and its systematic lagging behind industry; the closest
possible cooperation between science and technics, the
utmost encouragement of research work and the practical
application of its results on the widest possible social scale;
planned organization of scientific work; the application of
the most perfect methods of statistical accounting and
planned regulation of economy; the rapidly growing social
need, which is the most powerful internal driving force of
the whole system—all these will secure the maximum productivity of social labor, which in turn will release human
energy for the powerful development of science and art.

The development of the productive forces of world Communist society will make it possible to raise the well-being
of the whole of humanity and to reduce to a minimum the
time devoted to material production and, consequently,
will enable culture to flourish as never before in history.
This new culture of a humanity that is united for the first
time in history, and has abolished all State boundaries, will,
unlike capitalist culture, be based upon clear and trans-
parent human relationships. Hence, it will bury forever all
mysticism, religion, prejudice and superstition and will give
a powerful impetus to the development of all-conquering
scientific knowledge.

This higher stage of Communism, the stage in which
Communist society has already developed on its own foundation, in which an enormous growth of social productive

181

forces has accompanied the manifold development of man, in which humanity has already inscribed on its banner: "From each according to his abilities to each according to his needs!"—presupposes, as an historical condition precedent, a lower stage of development, the stage of Socialism. At this lower stage, Communist society only just emerges from capitalist society and bears all the economic, ethical and intellectual birthmarks it has inherited from the society from whose womb it is just emerging. The productive forces of Socialism are not yet sufficiently developed to assure a distribution of the products of labor according to needs: these are distributed according to the amount of labor expended. Division of labor, i.e. the system whereby certain groups perform certain labor function, and especially the distinction between mental and manual labor, still exists. Although classes are abolished, traces of the old class division of society and, consequently, remnants of the Proletarian State power, coercion, laws, still exist. Consequently, certain traces of inequality, which have not yet managed to die out altogether, still remain. The antagonism between town and country has not yet been entirely removed. But none of these survivals of former society is protected or defended by any social force. Being the product of a definite level of development of productive forces, they will disappear as rapidly as mankind, freed from the fetters of the capitalist system, subjugates the forces of nature, re-educates itself in the spirit of Communism, and passes from Socialism to complete Communism.

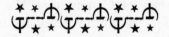

IV

THE PERIOD OF TRANSITION
FROM CAPITALISM TO SOCIALISM
AND THE DICTATORSHIP
OF THE PROLETARIAT

1. The Transition Period
and the Conquest of Power by the Proletariat

BETWEEN CAPITALIST SOCIETY and Communist society a period of revolutionary transformation intervenes, during which the one changes into the other. Correspondingly, there is also an intervening period of political transition, in which the essential State form is the Revolutionary Dictatorship of the Proletariat. The transition from the world dictatorship of imperialism to the world dictatorship of the proletariat extends over a long period of proletarian struggles with defeats as well as victories; a period of continuous general crises in capitalist relationships and growth of social revolutions, i.e. of proletarian civil wars against the bourgeoisie; a period of national wars and colonial rebellions which, although not in themselves revolutionary proletarian Socialist movements are nevertheless, objectively, insofar as they undermine the domination of imperialism, constituent parts of the world proletarian revolution; a period in which capitalist and socialist economic and social systems exist side by side in "peaceful" relationships as well as in armed conflict; a period of formation of a Union of Soviet Republics; a period of wars of Imperialist

183

States against Soviet States; a period in which the ties between the Soviet States and colonial peoples become more and more closely established, etc.

Uneven economic and political development is an abso-lute law of capitalism. This unevenness is still more pro-nounced and acute in the epoch of imperialism. Hence, it follows that the international proletarian revolution cannot be conceived as a single event occurring simultaneously all over the world; at first Socialism may be victorious in a few, or even in one single capitalist country. Every such prole-tarian victory, however, broadens the basis of the world revolution and consequently, still further intensifies the general crisis of capitalism. Thus, the capitalist system as a whole reaches the point of its final collapse; the dictatorship of finance capital perishes and gives place to the dictatorship of the proletariat.

Bourgeois revolutions brought about the political libera-tion of a system of productive relationships that had already established itself and become economically dominant, and transferred political power from the hands of one class of exploiters to the hands of another. Proletarian revolution, however, signifies the forcible invasion of the proletariat into the domain of property relationships of bourgeois society, the expropriation of the expropriating classes, and the transference of power to a class that aims at the radical reconstruction of the economic foundations of society and the abolition of all exploitation of man by man. The politi-cal domination of the feudal barons all over the world was broken in a series of separate bourgeois revolutions that extended over a period of centuries. The international pro-letarian revolution, however, although it will not be a single simultaneous act, but one extending over a whole epoch, nevertheless—thanks to the closer ties that now exist between the countries of the world, will accomplish its mission in a much shorter period of time. Only after the proletariat has achieved victory and consolidated its power all over the world will a prolonged period of intensive construction of world socialist economy set in.

The conquest of power by the Proletariat is a necessary condition precedent to the growth of Socialist forms of economy and to the cultural growth of the proletariat, which changes its own nature, perfects itself for the leadership of society in all spheres of life, draws into this process of transformation all other classes and thus prepares the ground for the abolition of classes altogether.

In the struggle for the dictatorship of the proletariat, and later for the transformation of the social system, as against the alliance of capitalists and landlords an alliance of workers and peasants is formed, under the intellectual and political hegemony of the former, an alliance which serves as the basis for the dictatorship of the proletariat.

The characteristic feature of the transition period as a whole, is the ruthless suppression of the resistance of the exploiters, the organization of Socialist construction, the mass training of men and women in the spirit of Socialism and the gradual disappearance of classes. Only to the extent that these great historical tasks are fulfilled will society of the transition period become transformed into Communist society.

Thus, the dictatorship of the world proletariat is an essential and vital condition precedent to the transition of world capitalist economy to socialist economy. This world dictatorship can be established only when the victory of Socialism has been achieved in certain countries or groups of countries, when the newly established proletarian republics enter into a federal union with the already existing prole-

185

tarian republics, when the number of such federations has grown and extended also to the colonies which have emancipated themselves from the yoke of imperialism; when these federations of republics have finally grown into a world union of Soviet Socialist Republics uniting the whole of mankind under the hegemony of the international proletariat organized as a State.

The conquest of power by the proletariat does not mean peacefully "capturing" the ready made bourgeois State machinery by means of a parliamentary majority. The bourgeoisie resorts to every means of violence and terror to safeguard and strengthen its predatory property and its political domination. Like the feudal nobility of the past, the bourgeoisie cannot abandon its historical position to the new class without a desperate and frantic struggle. Hence, the violence of the bourgeoisie can be suppressed only by the stern violence of the proletariat. The conquest of power by the proletariat is the violent overthrow of bourgeois power, the destruction of the capitalist State apparatus (bourgeois armies, police, bureaucratic hierarchy, the judiciary, parliaments, etc.) and substituting in its place new organs of proletarian power, to serve primarily as instruments for the suppression of the exploiters.

2. The Dictatorship of the Proletariat
and Its Soviet Form

As has been shown by the experience of the October Revolution of 1917 and by the Hungarian Revolution, which immeasurably enlarged the experience of the Paris

Commune of 1871, the most suitable form of proletarian State, is the Soviet State—a new type of State, which differs in principle from the bourgeois State, not only in its class content, but also in its internal structure. This is precisely the type of State which, emerging as it does directly out of the broadest possible mass movement of the toilers, secures the maximum of mass activity and is, consequently, the surest guarantee of final victory.

The Soviet form of State, being the highest form of democracy, namely, proletarian democracy, is the very opposite of bourgeois democracy, which is bourgeois dictatorship in a masked form. The Soviet State is the dictatorship of the proletariat, the rule of a single class—the proletriat. Unlike bourgeois democracy, proletarian democracy openly admits its class character and aims avowedly at the suppression of the exploiters in the interests of the overwhelming majority of the population. It deprives its class enemies of political rights and, under special historical conditions, may grant the proletariat a number of temporary advantages over the diffused petty-bourgeois peasantry in order to strengthen its role of leader. While disarming and suppressing its class enemies, the proletarian State at the same time regards this deprivation of political rights and partial restriction of liberty as temporary measures in the struggle against the attempts on the part of the exploiters to defend or restore their privileges. It inscribes on its banner the motto: the proletariat holds power not for the purpose of perpetuating it, not for the purpose of protecting narrow craft and professional interests, but for the purpose of uniting the backward and scattered rural proletariat, the semi-proletariat and the toiling peasants still more closely with the more progressive strata of the workers, for the purpose of gradually and systematically overcoming

187

class divisions altogether. Being an all-embracing form of the unity and organization of the masses under the leadership of the proletariat, the Soviets, in actual fact, draw the broad masses of the proletariat, the peasants and all toilers into the struggle for Socialism, into the work of building up Socialism and into the practical administration of the State; in the whole of their work they rely upon the working class organizations and practice the principles of broad democracy among the toilers to a far greater extent and immeasurably closer to the masses than any other form of government. The right of electing and recalling delegates, the combination of the executive with the legislative power, the electoral system based on a production and not on a residential qualification (election by workshops, factories, etc.) —all this secures for the working class and for the broad masses of the toilers who march under its hegemony, systematic, continuous and active participation in all public affairs—economic, social, political, military and cultural— and marks the sharp difference that exists between the bourgeois-parliamentary republic and the Soviet dictatorship of the proletariat.

Bourgeois democracy, with its formal equality of all citizens before the law, is in reality based on a glaring material and economic inequality of classes. By leaving inviolable, defending and strengthening the monopoly of the capitalist and landlord classes in the vital means of production, bourgeois democracy, as far as the exploited classes and especially the proletariat is concerned, converts this formal equality before the law and these democratic rights and liberties, which in practice are systematically curtailed, into a juridical fiction and, consequently, into a means for deceiving and enslaving the masses. Being the expression of the political domination of the bourgeoisie, so-called democracy is therefore capitalist democracy. By depriving the exploiting classes of the means of production, by placing the monopoly of these means of production in the hands of the proletariat as the dominant class in society, the Soviet State, first and foremost guarantees to the working class and to the toilers generally the material conditions for the exercise of their rights by providing them with premises, public buildings, printing plants, travelling facilities, etc.

In the domain of general political rights the Soviet State, while depriving the exploiters and the enemies of the people of political rights, completely abolishes for the first time all inequality of citizenship, which under systems of exploitation is based on distinctions of sex, religion and nationality; in this sphere it establishes an equality that is not to be found in any bourgeois country. In this respect also, the dictatorship of the proletariat steadily lays down the material basis upon which this equality may be truly exercised by introducing measures for the emancipation of women, the industrialization of former colonies, etc.

Soviet democracy, therefore, is proletarian democracy, democracy of the toiling masses, democracy directed against the exploiters.

The Soviet State completely disarms the bourgeoisie and concentrates all arms in the hands of the proletariat; it is the armed proletarian State. The armed forces under the Soviet State are organized on a class basis, which corresponds to the general structure of the proletarian dictatorship, and guarantees the role of leadership to the industrial proletariat. This organization, while maintaining revolutionary discipline, ensures to the warriors of the Red Army and Navy close and constant contacts with the masses of the toilers, participation in the administration of the country and in the work of building up Socialism.

3. *The Dictatorship and the Proletariat and the Expropriation of the Expropriators*

The victorious proletariat utilizes the conquest of power as a lever of economic revolution, i. e. the revolutionary transformation of the property relations of capitalism into relationships of the Socialist mode of production. The starting point of this great economic revolution is the expropriation of the landlords and capitalists, i. e. the conversion of the monopolistic property of the bourgeoisie into the property of the proletarian State.

In this sphere the Communist International advances the following fundamental tasks of the proletarian dictatorship:

A. INDUSTRY, TRANSPORT AND COMMUNICATION SERVICES

a) The confiscation and proletarian nationalization of all large private capitalist undertakings (factories, works, mines and electric power stations) and the transference of all State and municipal enterprises to the Soviets.

b) The confiscation and proletarian nationalization of private capitalist railway, waterway, automobile and air transport services (commercial and passenger air fleet) and the transference of all State and municipal transport services to the Soviets.

c) The confiscation and proletarian nationalization of private capitalist communication services (telegraphs, telephones and wireless) and the transference of State and municipal communication services to the Soviets.

d) The organization of workers' management of industry. The establishment of State organs for the management of industry with provision for the close participation of the trade unions in this work of management. Appropriate functions to be guaranteed for the factory and works councils.

e) Industrial activity to be directed towards the satisfaction of the needs of the broad masses of the toilers. The reorganization of the branches of industry that formerly served the needs of the ruling class (luxury, trades, etc.). The strengthening of the branches of industry that will facilitate the development of agriculture, with the object of strengthening the ties between industry and peasant economy, of facilitating the development of State farms, and of accelerating the rate of development of national economy as a whole.

B.   AGRICULTURE

a) The confiscation and proletarian nationalization of all large landed estates in town and country (private, church, monastery and other lands) and the transference of State and municipal landed property including forests, minerals, lakes, rivers, etc., to the Soviets with subsequent nationalization of the whole of the land.

b) The confiscation of all property utilized in production belonging to large landed estates, such as: buildings, machinery and other inventory, cattle, enterprises for the manufacture of agricultural products (large flour mills, cheese plants, dairy farms, fruit and vegetable drying plants, etc.).

c) The transfer of large estates, particularly model estates and those of considerable economic importance to the management of the organs of the proletarian dictatorship and of the Soviet farm organizations.

191

d) Part of the land confiscated from the landlords and others, particularly where the land was cultivated by the peasants on a tenant basis and served as a means of holding the peasantry in economic bondage—to be transferred to the use of the peasantry (to the poor and partly also to the middle strata of the peasantry). The amount of land to be so transferred to be determined by economic expediency as well as by the degree of necessity to neutralize the peasantry and to win them over to the side of the proletariat; this amount must necessarily vary according to the different circumstances.

e) Prohibition of buying and selling of land, as a means of preserving the land for the peasantry and preventing its passing into the hands of capitalists, land speculators, etc. Offenders against this law to be severly prosecuted.

f) To combat usury. All transactions entailing terms of bondage to be annulled. All debts of the exploited strata of the peasantry to be annulled. The poorest stratum of the peasantry to be relieved from taxation, etc.

g) Comprehensive State measures for developing the productive forces of agriculture; the development of rural electrification; the manufacture of tractors, the production of artificial fertilizers; the production of pure quality seeds and raising thoroughbred stock on Soviet farms; the extensive organization of agricultural credits for land reclamation, etc.

h) Financial and other support for agricultural co-operation and for all forms of collective production in the rural districts (co-operative societies, communes, etc.). Systematic propaganda in favor of peasant co-operation (selling, credit and supply co-operative societies) to be based on the mass activity of the peasants themselves; propaganda in favor of the transition to large-scale agricultural production

192

which—owing to the undoubted technical and economic advantages of large-scale production—provide the greatest immediate economic gain and also a method of transition to Socialism most accessible to the broad masses of the toiling peasants.

C. TRADE AND CREDIT

a) The proletarian nationalization of private banks (the entire gold reserve, all securities, deposits, etc. to be transferred to the Proletarian State); the proletarian State to take over State, Municipal, etc., banks.

b) The centralization of banking; all nationalized big banks to be subordinated to the central State bank.

c) The nationalization of wholesale trade and large retail trading enterprizes (warehouses, elevators, stores, stocks of goods, etc.), and their transfer to the organs of the Soviet State.

d) Every encouragement to be given to consumers' cooperatives as representing an integral part of the distributing apparatus, while maintaining uniformity in their system of work and securing the active participation of the masses themselves in their work.

e) The monopoly of foreign trade.

f) The repudiation of State debts to foreign and home capitalists.

D. CONDITIONS OF LIFE, LABOR, ETC.

a) Reduction of the working day to seven hours, and to six hours in industries particularly harmful to the health of the workers. Further reduction of the working day and transition to a five-day week in countries with developed productive forces. The regulation of the working day to correspond to the increase of the productivity of labor.

b) Prohibition, as a rule, of night work and employment in harmful trades for all females. Prohibition of child labor. Prohibition of overtime.

c) Special reduction of the work-day for the youth (a maximum six hour day for young persons up to 18 years of age). Socialistic reorganization of the labor of young persons so as to combine employment in industry with general and political education.

d) Social insurance in all forms (sickness, old age, accident, unemployment, etc.) at State expense (and at the expense of the owners of private enterprises where they still exist), insurance affairs to be managed by the insured themselves.

e) Comprehensive measures of hygiene; the organization of free medical service. To combat social diseases (alcoholism, venereal diseases, tuberculosis, etc.).

f) Complete equality between men and women before the law and in social life; a radical reform of marital and family laws; recognition of maternity as a social function; protection of mothers and infants. Initiation of social care and upbringing of infants and children (creches, kindergartens, children's homes, etc.).

The establishment of institutions that will gradually relieve the burden of house drudgery (public kitchens and laundries), and systematic cultural struggle against the ideology and traditions of female bondage.

E. HOUSING

a) The confiscation of big house property.
b) The transfer of confiscated houses to the administra-

tion of the local Soviets.

c) Workers to be removed to bourgeois residential districts.

d) Palaces and large private and public buildings to be placed at the disposal of labor organizations.

e) The carrying out of an extensive program of house construction.

F. NATIONAL AND COLONIAL QUESTIONS

a) The recognition of the right of all nations, irrespective of race, to complete self-determination, that is, self-determination inclusive of the right to State separation.

b) The voluntary unification and centralization of the military and economic forces of all nations, liberated from capitalism for the purpose of fighting against imperialism and for building up Socialist economy.

c) Wide and determined struggle against the imposition of any kind of limitation and restriction upon any nationality, nation or race. Complete equality for all nations and races.

d) The Soviet State to guarantee and support with all the resources at its command the national cultures of nations liberated from capitalism, at the same time to carry out a consistent proletarian policy directed towards the development of the content of such cultures.

e) Every assistance to be rendered to the economic, political and cultural growth of the formerly oppressed "territories," "dominions" and "colonies," with the object of transferring them to Socialist lines, so that a durable basis may be laid for complete national equality.

f) To combat all remnants of chauvinism, national

hatred, race prejudices and other ideological products of feudal and capitalist barbarism.

G. MEANS OF IDEOLOGICAL INFLUENCE

a) The nationalization of printing plants.

b) The monopoly of newspaper and book-publishing.

c) The nationalization of big cinema enterprises, theatres, etc.

d) The utilization of the nationalized means of "intellectual production" for the most extensive political and general education of the toilers and for the building up of a new Socialist culture on a proletarian class basis.

4. *The Basis for the Economic Policy of the Proletarian Dictatorship*

In carrying out all these tasks of the dictatorship of the proletariat, the following postulates must be borne in mind:

1. The complete abolition of private property in land, and the nationalization of the land, cannot be brought about immediately in the more developed capitalist countries, where the principle of private property is deep-rooted among broad strata of the peasantry. In such countries, the nationalization of all the land can only be brought about gradually, by means of a series of transitional measures.

2. Nationalization of production should not, as a rule, be applied to small and middle-sized enterprises (peasants, small artisans, handicraft, small and medium shops, small manufacturers, etc.). Firstly, because the proletariat must

draw a strict distinction between the property of the small commodity producer working for himself, who can and must be gradually brought into the groove of Socialist construction, and the property of the capitalist exploiter, the liquidation of which is an essential condition precedent for Socialist construction.

Secondly, because the proletariat, after seizing power, may not have sufficient organizing forces at its disposal, particularly in the first phases of the dictatorship, for the purpose of destroying capitalism and at the same time to establish contacts with the smaller and medium individual units of production on a Socialist basis. These small individual enterprises (primarily peasant enterprises) will be drawn into the general Socialist organization of production and distribution only gradually, with the powerful and systematic aid the proletarian State will render to organize them in all the various forms of collective enterprises. Any attempt to break up their economic system violently and to compel them to adopt collective methods by force will only lead to harmful results.

3. Owing to the prevalence of a large number of small units of production (primarily peasant farms, farmers' enterprises, small artisans, small shopkeepers, etc.) in colonies, semi-colonies and economically backward countries, where the petty-bourgeois masses represent the overwhelming majority of the population, and even in centers of capitalist world industry (the United States of America, Germany, and to some degree also England), it is necessary, in the first stage of development to preserve to some extent, market forms of economic contacts, the money system, etc. The variety of prevailing economic forms (ranging from Socialist large scale industry to small peasant and artisan enterprises), which unavoidably come into conflict with each

other; the variety of classes and class groups corresponding to this variety of economic forms, each having different stimuli for economic activity and conflicting class interests, and finally, the prevalence in all spheres of economic life, of habits and traditions inherited from bourgeois activity, which cannot be removed all at once—all this demands that the proletariat, in exercising its economic leadership, shall properly combine, on the basis of market relationships, large-scale Socialist industry with the small enterprises of the simple commodity producers, i.e., it must combine them in such a way as to guarantee the leading role to Socialist industry and at the same time bring about the greatest possible development of the mass of peasant enterprises. Hence, the greater the weight of importance of scattered, small peasant labor in the general economy of the country, the greater will be the extent of market relations, the smaller will be the significance of directly planned management, and the greater will be the degree to which the general economic plan will depend upon forecasts of uncontrollable economic relations. On the other hand, the smaller the weight of importance of small production, the greater will be the proportion of socialized labor, the more powerful will be the concentrated and socialized means of production, the smaller will be the extent of market relations, the greater will be the importance of planned management as compared with uncoordinated management and the more considerable and universal will be the application of planned management in the sphere of production and distribution.

Provided the proletarian dictatorship carries out a correct class policy—i. e. provided proper account is taken of class-relationships—the technical and economic superiority of large-scale socialized production, the centralization of all the most important economic key positions (industry, transport, large-scale agricultural enterprises, banks, etc.) in the hands of the proletarian State, planned management of industry, and the power wielded by the State apparatus as a whole (the budget, taxes, administrative legislation and legislation generally), render it possible continuously and systematically to dislodge private capital and the new out-crops of capitalism which, in the period of more or less free commercial and market relations emerge in town and coun-try with the development of simple commodity production (big farmers, kulaks). At the same time, by organizing peas-ant farming on co-operative lines, and as a result of the growth of collective forms of economy, the great bulk of the peasant enterprises will be systematically drawn into the main channel of developing Socialism. The outwardly capi-talistic forms and methods of economic activity that are bound up with market relations (money form of account-ing, payment for labor in money, buying and selling, credit and banks, etc.), serve as levers for the Socialist transforma-tion, insofar as they to an increasing degree serve the con-sistently Socialist type of enterprises, i.e. the Socialist sec-tion of economy.

Thus provided the State carries out a correct policy, market relations under the proletarian dictatorship destroy themselves in the process of their own development by helping to dislodge private capital, by changing the char-acter of peasant economy—what time the means of produc-tion become more and more centralized and concentrated in the hands of the proletarian State—they help to destroy market relations altogether.

In the event of probable capitalist military intervention, and of prolonged counter-revolutionary wars against the dictatorship of the proletariat, the necessity may arise for a war-Communist economic policy ("War Communism"), which is nothing more nor less than the organization of rational consumption for the purpose of military defense, accompanied by a system of intensified pressure upon the capitalist groups (confiscation, requisitions, etc.), with the more or less complete liquidation of freedom of trade and market relations and a sharp disturbance of the individualistic, economic stimuli of the small producers, which results in a diminution of the productive forces of the country. This policy of "War Communism," while it undermines the material basis of the strata of the population in the country that are hostile to the working class, secures a rational distribution of the available supplies and facilitates the military struggle of the proletarian dictatorship—which is the historical justification of this policy—nevertheless, cannot be regarded as the "normal" economic policy of the proletarian dictatorship.

5. Dictatorship of the Proletariat and the Classes

The dictatorship of the proletariat is a continuation of the class struggle under new conditions. The dictatorship of the proletariat is a stubborn fight—bloody and bloodless, violent and peaceful, military and economic, pedagogical and administrative—against the forces and traditions of the old society, against external capitalist enemies, against the remnants of the exploiting classes within the country, against the upshoots of the new bourgeoisie that spring up on the basis of still prevailing commodity production.

After the civil war has been brought to an end the stubborn class struggle continues in new forms, primarily, in the form of a struggle between the survivals of previous economic systems and fresh upshoots of them on the one hand, and Socialist forms of economy on the other. The forms of the struggle undergo a change at various stages of Socialist development, and in the first stages, the struggle, under certain conditions, may be extremely severe.

In the initial stage of the proletarian dictatorship, the policy of the proletariat towards other classes and social groups within the country is determined by the following postulates:

1. The big bourgeoisie and the landowners, a section of the officer corps, the higher command of the forces, and the higher bureaucracy—who remain loyal to the bourgeoisie and the landlords—are consistent enemies of the working class against whom ruthless war must be waged. The organizing skill of a certain section of these strata may be utilized, but as a rule, only after the dictatorship has been consolidated and all conspiracies and rebellions of exploiters have been decisively crushed.

2. In regard to the technical intelligentsia, which was brought up in the spirit of bourgeois traditions and the higher ranks of which were closely linked up with the commanding apparatus of capital, the proletariat, while ruthlessly suppressing every counter-revolutionary action on the part of hostile sections of the intelligentsia, must at the same time give consideration to the necessity of utilizing this skilled social force for the work of Socialist construction; it must give every encouragement to the groups that are neutral, and especially to those that are friendly, towards the proletarian revolution. In widening the economic, technical and cultural perspectives of Socialist construction to its utmost social limits, the proletariat must systematically win over the technical intelligentsia to its side, subject it to its ideological influence and secure its close co-operation in

the work of social reconstruction.

3. In regard to the peasantry, the task of the Communist Parties, is, while placing its reliance in the agricultural proletariat, to win over all the exploited and toiling strata of the countryside. The victorious proletariat must draw strict distinctions between the various groups among the peasantry, weigh their relative importance, and render every support to the propertyless and semi-proletarian sections of the peasantry by transferring to them a part of the land taken from the big landowners and by helping them in their struggle against usurer's capital, etc. Moreover, the proletariat must neutralize the middle strata of the peasantry and mercilessly suppress the slightest opposition on the part of the village bourgeoisie who ally themselves with the landowners. As its dictatorship becomes consolidated and Socialist construction develops, the proletariat must proceed from the policy of neutralization to a policy of durable alliance with the masses of middle peasantry, but must not adopt the viewpoint of sharing power in any form. The dictatorship of the proletariat implies that the industrial workers alone are capable of leading the entire mass of the toilers. On the other hand, while representing the rule of a single class, the dictatorship of the proletariat at the same time represents a special form of class alliance between the proletariat, as the vanguard of the toilers, and the numerous non-proletarian sections of the toiling masses, or the majority of them. It represents an alliance for the complete overthrow of capital, for the complete suppression of the opposition of the bourgeoisie and its attempts at restoration, an alliance aiming at the complete building up and consolidation of Socialism.

4. The petty urban bourgeoisie, which continuously wavers between extreme reaction and sympathy for the

proletariat, must likewise be neutralized and, as far as possible, won over to the side of the proletariat. This can be achieved by leaving to them their small property and permitting a certain measure of free trade, by releasing them from the bondage of usurious credit and by the proletariat helping them in all sorts of ways in the struggle against all and every form of capitalist oppression.

6. Mass Organizations
in the System of Proletarian Dictatorship

In the process of fulfilling these tasks of the proletarian dictatorship, a radical change takes place in the tasks and functions of the mass organizations, particularly of the labor organizations. Under capitalism, the mass labor organizations, in which the broad masses of the proletariat were originally organized and trained, i. e. the trade (industrial) unions, serve as the principal weapons in struggle against trustified capital and its State. Under the proletarian dictatorship, they become transformed into the principal lever of the State; they become transformed into a school of Communism, by means of which vast masses of the proletariat are drawn into the work of Socialist management of production; they are transformed into organizations directly connected with all parts of the State apparatus, influencing all branches of its work, safeguarding the permanent and day to day interests of the working class and fighting against bureaucracy in the departments of the State. Thus, in so far as they promote from their ranks leaders in the work of construction, draw into this work of construction broad sections of the proletariat and aim at combating bureaucracy, which inevitably arises as a result of the operation of class influences alien to the proletariat and of the inadequate cultural development of the masses, the trade unions become the backbone of the proletarian economic and State organization as a whole.

Notwithstanding reformist utopias, working class cooperative organizations under capitalism are doomed to play a very minor role and in the general environment of the capitalist system not infrequently degenerate into mere appendages of capitalism. Under the dictatorship of the proletariat, however, these organizations can and must become the most important units of the distributing Apparatus.

Lastly, peasant agricultural co-operative organizations (selling, purchasing, credit and producing), under proper management and provided a systematic struggle is carried on against the capitalist elements, and that really broad masses of the toilers who follow the lead of the proletariat take a really active part in their work, can and must become one of the principal organizational means for linking up town and country. To the extent that they were able to maintain their existence at all under capitalism, co-operative peasant enterprises inevitably became transformed into capitalist enterprises, for they were dependent upon capitalist industry, capitalist banks and upon capitalist economic environment. Under the dictatorship of the proletariat, however, such enterprises develop amidst a different system of relationships, depend upon proletarian industry, proletarian banks, etc. Thus, provided the proletariat carries out a proper policy, provided the class struggle is systematically conducted against the capitalist elements outside as well as inside the co-operative organizations, and provided Socialist

industry exercises its guidance over it, agricultural co-operation will become one of the principal levers for the Socialist
transformation and collectivization of the countryside. All
this, however, does not exclude the possibility that in certain
countries the consumers' societies, and particularly the agricultural co-operative societies led by the bourgeoisie and
their Social-Democratic agents, will at first be hotbeds of
counter-revolutionary activity and sabotage against the work
of economic construction of the workers' revolution.

In the course of this militant and constructive work, carried on through the medium of these multifarious proletarian organizations—which should serve as effective levers
of the Soviet State and the link between it and the masses
of all strata of the working class—the proletariat secures
unity of will and action and exercises this unity through the
medium of the Communist Party, which plays the leading
role in the system of the proletarian dictatorship.

The Party of the proletariat relies directly on the trade
unions and other organizations that embrace the masses
of the workers, and through these, relies on the peasantry
(Soviets, co-operative societies, Young Communist League,
etc.); by means of these levers it guides the whole Soviet
system. The proletariat can fulfill its role as organizer of the
new society only if the Soviet government is loyally supported by all the mass organizations, only if class unity is
maintained, and only under the guidance of the Party.

7. *The Dictatorship of the Proletariat
and the Cultural Revolution*

The role of organizer of the new human society pre-

205

supposes that the proletariat itself will become culturally mature, that it will transform its own nature, that it will continually promote from its ranks increasing numbers of men and women capable of mastering science, technics and administration in order to build up Socialism and a new Socialist culture.

Bourgeois revolution against feudalism presupposes that a new class has arisen in the midst of feudal society that is culturally more advanced than the ruling class and is already the dominant factor in economic life. The proletarian revolution, however, develops under other conditions. Being economically exploited, politically oppressed and culturally downtrodden under capitalism, the working class transforms its own nature only in the course of the transition period, only after it has conquered State power, only by destroying the bourgeois monopoly of education and mastering all the sciences, and only after it has gained experience in great works of construction. The mass awakening of Communist consciousness, the cause of Socialism itself, calls for a mass change of human nature, which can be achieved only in the course of the practical movement, in revolution. Hence, revolution is not only necessary because there is no other way of overthrowing the ruling class, but also because, only in the process of revolution is the overthrowing class able to purge itself of the dross of the old society and become capable of creating a new society.

In destroying the capitalist monopoly of the means of production, the working class must also destroy the capitalist monopoly of education, that is, it must take possession of all the schools, from the elementary schools to the universities. It is particularly important for the proletariat to train members of the working class as experts in the sphere of production (engineers, technicians, organizers, etc.), as well as in the sphere of military affairs, science, art, etc. Parallel with this work stands the task of raising the general cultural level of the proletarian masses, of improving their political education, of raising their general standard of knowledge and technical skill, of training them in the methods of public work and administration, and of combating the survivals of bourgeois and petty-bourgeois prejudices, etc.

Only to the extent that the proletarian promotes from its own ranks a body of men and women capable of occupying the "key positions" of Socialist construction, only to the extent that this body grows, and draws increasing numbers of the working class into the process of revolutionary-cultural transformation and gradually obliterates the line that divides the proletariat into an "advanced" and a "backward" section will the guarantees be created for successful Socialist construction and against bureaucratic decay and class degeneracy.

However, in the process of revolution the proletariat not only changes its own nature, but also the nature of other classes, primarily the numerous petty-bourgeois strata in town and country and especially the toiling sections of the peasantry. By drawing the wide masses into the process of cultural revolution and Socialist construction, by uniting and Communistically educating them with all the means at its disposal, by strongly combating all anti-proletarian and narrow craft ideologies, and by persistently and systematically overcoming the general and cultural backwardness of the rural districts, the working class, on the basis of the developing collective forms of economy, prepares the way for the complete removal of class divisions in society.

One of the most important tasks of the cultural revolution affecting the wide masses, is the task of systematically and unswervingly combating religion—the opium of the people. The proletarian government must withdraw all State support from the Church, which is the agency of the former ruling class; it must prevent all church interference in State-organized educational affairs, and ruthlessly suppress the counter-revolutionary activity of the ecclesiastical organizations. At the same time, the proletarian State, while granting liberty of worship and abolishing the privileged position of the formerly dominant religion, carries on anti-religious propaganda with all the means at its command and reconstructs the whole of its educational work on the basis of scientific materialism.

8. The Struggle for the World Dictatorship
of the Proletariat
and the Principal Types of Revolutions

The international proletarian revolution represents a combination of processes which vary in time and character; purely proletarian revolutions; revolutions of a bourgeois-democratic type which grow into proletarian revolutions; wars for national liberation; colonial revolutions. The World Dictatorship of the Proletariat comes only as the final result of the revolutionary process.

The uneven development of capitalism, which became more accentuated in the period of imperialism, has given rise to a variety of types of capitalism, to different stages of ripeness of capitalism in different countries, and to a variety of specific conditions of the revolutionary process. These circumstances make it historically inevitable that the proletariat will come to power by a variety of ways and degrees of rapidity; that a number of countries must pass through certain transition stages leading to the dictatorship of the proletariat and must adopt varied forms of Socialist construction.

The variety of conditions and ways by which the proletariat will achieve its dictatorship in the various countries may be divided schematically into three main types.

Countries of highly developed capitalism (United States of America, Germany, Great Britain, etc.), having powerful productive forces, highly centralized production, with small-scale production reduced to relative insignificance, and a long established bourgeois-democratic political system. In such countries the fundamental political demand of the program is direct transition to the dictatorship of the proletariat. In the economic sphere, the most characteristic demands are: expropriation of the whole of large-scale industry; organization of a large number of State Soviet farms and, in contrast to this, a relatively small portion of the land to be transferred to the peasantry; unregulated market relations to be given comparatively small scope; rapid rate of Socialist development generally, and of collectivization of peasant farming in particular.

Countries with a medium development of capitalism (Spain, Portugal, Poland, Hungary, the Balkan countries, etc.), having numerous survivals of semi-feudal relationships in agriculture, possessing, to a certain extent, the material prerequisites for Socialist construction, and in which the bourgeois-democratic reforms have not yet been completed. In some of these countries a process of more or less rapid development from bourgeois-democratic revolution to Socialist revolution is possible. In others, there may be types of proletarian revolutions which will have a large number of bourgeois-democratic tasks to fulfill. Hence, in these countries, the dictatorship of the proletariat may not come about at once, but in the process of transition from the democratic dictatorship of the proletariat and peasantry to the Socialist dictatorship of the proletariat; where the Revolution develops directly as a proletarian revolution it is presumed that the proletariat exercises leadership over a broad agrarian peasant movement. In general, the agrarian revolution plays a most important part in these countries, and in some cases a decisive role; in the process of expropriating large landed property a considerable portion of the confiscated land is placed at the disposal of the peasantry; the volume of market relations prevailing after the victory of the proletariat is considerable; the task of organizing the peasantry along co-operative lines and later, of combining them in production, occupies an important place among the tasks of Socialist construction. The rate of this construction is relatively slow.

Colonial and semi-colonial countries (China, India, etc.) and dependent countries (Argentina, Brazil, etc.), having the rudiments of and in some cases considerably developed industry, but in the majority of cases inadequate for independent Socialist construction; with feudal medieval relationships, or "Asiatic mode of production" relationships prevailing in their economics and in their poltical superstructure; and in which the principal industrial, commercial and banking enterprises, the principal means of transport, the large landed estates (latifundia), plantations, etc., are concentrated in the hands of foreign imperialist groups. The principal task in such countries is, on the one hand, to fight against feudalism and the pro-capitalist forms of exploitation and to develop systematically the peasant agrarian revolution; on the other hand, to fight against foreign imperialism and for national independence. As a rule, transition to the dictatorship of the proletariat in these countries will be possible only through a series of preparatory stages, as the outcome of a whole period of transformation of bourgeois-democratic revolution into Socialist revolution, while in the majority of cases, successful Socialist construction will be possible only if direct support is obtained from the countries in which the proletarian dictatorship is established.

In still more backward countries (as in some parts of Africa) where there are no wage workers or very few, where the majority of the population still live in tribal conditions, where survivals of primitive tribal forms still exist, where the national bourgeoisie is almost non-existent, where the primary role of foreign imperialism is that of military occupation and usurpation of land, the central task is to fight for national independence. Victorious national uprisings in these countries may open the way for their direct development towards Socialism and their avoiding the stage of capitalism, provided real, powerful assistance is rendered to them by the countries in which the proletarian dictatorship is established.

Thus, in the epoch in which the proletariat in the most developed capitalist countries is confronted with the immediate task of capturing power, in which the dictatorship of the proletariat is already established in the U.S.S.R. and is a factor of world significance, the movement for liberation in colonial and semi-colonial countries, which was brought into being by the penetration of world capitalism, may lead to socialist development—notwithstanding the immaturity of social relationship in these countries taken by themselves —provided they receive the assistance and support of the proletarian dictatorship and of the international proletarian movement generally.

9. Struggle for the World Dictatorship of the Proletariat and Colonial Revolution

The special conditions of the revolutionary struggle prevailing in colonial and semi-colonial countries, the inevitably long period of struggle required for the democratic dictatorship of the proletariat and the peasantry and for the transformation of this dictatorship into the dictatorship of the proletariat, and, finally, the decisive importance of the national aspects of the struggle, impose upon the Communist Parties of these countries a number of special tasks, which are preparatory stages to the general tasks of the dictatorship of the proletariat. The Communist International considers the following to be the most important of these special tasks:

1. To overthrow the rule of foreign imperialism, of the feudal rulers and of the landlord bureaucracy.

2. To establish the democratic dictatorship of the proletariat and the peasantry on a Soviet basis.

3. Complete national independence and national unification.

4. Annulment of State debts.

5. Nationalization of large-scale enterprises (industrial, transport, banking and others), owned by the imperialists.

6. The confiscation of landlord, church and monastery lands. The nationalization of all the land.

7. Introduction of the 8-hour day.

8. The organization of revolutionary workers' and peasants' armies.

In the colonies and semi-colonies where the proletariat is the leader of and commands hegemony in the struggle, the consistent bourgeois-democratic revolution will grow into proletarian revolution—in proportion as the struggle develops and becomes more intense (sabotage by the bourgeoisie, confiscation of the enterprises belonging to the sabotaging section of the bourgeoisie, which inevitably extends to the nationalization of the whole of large-scale industry). In the colonies where there is no proletariat, the overthrow of the domination of the imperialists implies the establishment of the rule of people's (peasant) Soviets, the confiscation and transfer to the State of foreign enterprises and lands.

Colonial revolutions and movements for national liberation play an extremely important part in the struggle against imperialism and in the struggle for the conquest of power by the working class. Colonies and semi-colonies are also important in the transition period because they represent the world rural district in relation to the industrial countries, which represent the world city. Consequently, the problem of organizing Socialist world economy, of properly combining industry with agriculture is, to a large extent, the problem of the relation towards the former colonies of imperialism. The establishment of a fraternal, militant alliance with the masses of the toilers in the colonies represents one of the principal tasks the world industrial proletariat must fulfill as leader in the struggle against imperialism.

Thus, in rousing the workers in the home countries for the struggle for the dictatorship of the proletariat, the progress of the world revolution also rouses hundreds of millions of colonial workers and peasants for the struggle against foreign imperialism. In view of the existence of centers of Socialism represented by Soviet Republics of growing economic power, the colonies which break away from imperialism economically gravitate towards and gradually combine

213

with the industrial centers of world Socialism, are drawn into the channel of Socialist construction, and by skipping the further stage of development of capitalism, as the predominant system, obtain opportunities for rapid economic and cultural progress. The Peasants' Soviets in the backward ex-colonies and the Workers' and Peasants' Soviets in the more developed ex-colonies group themselves politically around the centers of proletarian dictatorship, join the growing Federation of Soviet Republics, and thus enter the general system of the world proletarian dictatorship.

Socialism, as the new method of production, thus obtains world-wide scope of development.

V

THE DICTATORSHIP OF THE PROLETARIAT
IN THE INTERNATIONAL SOCIAL REVOLUTION

1. *The Building Up of Socialism in the U.S.S.R.*
and the Class Struggle

THE PRINCIPAL MANIFESTATION of the profound crisis of the capitalist system is the division of world economy into capitalist countries on the one hand, and countries building up Socialism on the other. Therefore, the internal consolidation of the proletarian dictatorship in the U.S.S.R., the success achieved in the work of Socialist construction, the growth of the influence and authority of the U.S.S.R., among the masses of the proletariat and the oppressed peoples of the colonies, signify, therefore, the continuation, intensification and expansion of the International Social Revolution.

Possessing in the country the necessary and sufficient material prerequisites not only for the overthrow of the landlords and the bourgeoisie, but also for the establishment of complete Socialism, the workers of the Soviet Republic, with the aid of the international proletariat, heroically repelled the attacks of the armed forces of the internal and foreign counter-revolution, consolidated their alliance with the bulk of the peasantry and achieved considerable success in the sphere of Socialist construction.

The contacts established between proletarian Socialist industry and small peasant economy, which stimulates the growth of the productive forces of agriculture and at the same time assures the leading role to Socialist industry; the

215

linking up of industry with agriculture in place of the former capitalist production for the satisfaction of the unproductive consumption of parasitic classes; production, not for capitalist profit, but for the satisfaction of the growing needs of the masses of the consumers; the growth of the needs of the masses, which in the final analysis greatly stimulates the entire productive process; and finally, the close concentration of the economic key positions under the command of the proletarian State, the growth of planned management and the more economic and expedient distribution of the means of production that goes with it—all this enables the proletariat to make rapid progress along the road of Socialist construction.

In raising the level of the productive forces of the whole economy of the country, and in steering a straight course for the industrialization of the U.S.S.R.—the rapidity of which is dictated by the international and internal situation, the proletariat in the U.S.S.R., notwithstanding the systematic attempts on the part of the capitalist Powers to organize an economic and financial boycott against the Soviet Republics, at the same time increases the relative share of the Socialized (Socialist) section of national economy in the total means of production in the country, in the total output of industry and in the total trade turnover.

Thus, with the land nationalized, by means of the levers of State trade and rapidly growing co-operation, and with the increasing industrialization of the country, State Socialist industry, transport and banking are more and more guiding the activities of the small and very small peasant enterprises.

In the sphere of agriculture especially, the level of the forces of production is being raised amidst conditions that restrict the process of differentiation among the peasantry (nationalization of the land, and consequently, the prohibi-

216

tion of the sale and purchase of land; sharply graded progressive taxation; the financing of poor and middle peasants' co-operative societies and producers' organizations; laws regulating the hiring of labor; depriving the kulaks of certain political and public rights; organizing the rural poor in separate organizations, etc.). However, insofar as the productive forces of Socialist industry have not yet grown sufficiently to enable a broad, new technical base to be laid for agriculture and, consequently, to render possible the immediate and rapid unification of peasant enterprises into large public enterprises (collective farms), the kulak class tends to grow and establish, first economic, and then political contacts with the elements of the so-called "new bourgeoisie."

Being in command of the principal economic key positions in the country and systematically squeezing out the remnants of urban and private capital, which has greatly dwindled in the last few years of the "New Economic Policy"; restricting in every way the exploiting strata in the rural districts that arise out of the development of commodity and money relationships; supporting existing Soviet farms in the rural districts and establishing new ones; drawing the bulk of the peasant simple commodity producers, through the medium of rapidly growing co-operative organizations, into the general system of Soviet economic organization, and consequently into the work of Socialist construction, which in the conditions prevailing under the proletarian dictatorship and with the economic leadership of Socialist industry is identical with the development of Socialism; passing from the process of restoration to the process of expanded reproduction of the entire productive and technical base of the country—the proletariat of the U.S.S.R. sets itself, and is already beginning to fulfill the task of large-scale capital construction (production of means

217

of production generally, development of heavy industry and especially of electrification) and, developing still further, selling, buying and credit co-operation, sets itself the task of organizing the peasantry in producing co-operatives on a mass scale and on a collectivist basis, which calls for the powerful material assistance of the Proletarian State.

Thus, being already a decisive economic force determining, in the main, the entire economic development of the U.S.S.R., Socialism, by that very fact, makes still further strides in its development and systematically overcomes the difficulties that arise from the petty-bourgeois character of the country and the periods of temporarily acute class antagonisms.

The task of re-equipping industry and the need for large investments in capital construction, unavoidably give rise to serious difficulties in the path of Socialist development which, in the last analysis, are to be attributed to the technical and economic backwardness of the country and to the ruin caused in the years of the imperialist and civil wars. Notwithstanding this, however, the standard of living of the working class and of the broad masses of the toilers is steadily rising and, simultaneously with the Socialist rationalization and scientific organization of industry, the 7-hour day is gradually being introduced, which opens up still wider prospects for the improvement of the conditions of life and labor of the working class.

Standing on the basis of the economic growth of the U.S.S.R. and on the steady increase in the relative importance of the Socialist section of its economy; never for a moment halting in the struggle against the kulaks; relying upon the rural poor and maintaining a firm alliance with the bulk of the middle peasantry, the working class, united and led by the Communist Party, which has been hardened in revolutionary battles, draws increasing masses, scores of millions of toilers into the work of Socialist construction. The principal means employed towards this aim are: the development of broad mass organizations (the Party, as the guiding force; the trade unions, as the backbone of the entire system of the proletarian dictatorship; the Young Communist League; co-operative societies of all types; working women's and peasant women's organizations; the various so-called "voluntary societies"; worker and peasant correspondents' societies; sport, scientific, cultural and educational organizations); full encouragement of the initiative of the masses and the promotion of fresh strata of workers to high posts in all spheres of industry and administration. The steady attraction of the masses into the process of Socialist construction, the constant renovation of the entire State, economic, trade union and Party apparatus with men and women fresh from the ranks of the proletariat, the systematic training, in the higher educational establishments and at special courses, of workers generally and young workers in particular as new, Socialist experts in all branches of construction—all these together serve as one of the principal guarantees against the bureaucratic ossification or social degeneration of the stratum of the proletariat directly engaged in administration.

2. *The Significance of the U.S.S.R.*
and Her World Revolutionary Duties

Having defeated Russian imperialism and liberated all the former colonies and oppressed nations of the Tsarist

219

Empire, and systematically laying a firm foundation for their cultural and political development by industrializing their territories; having guaranteed the juridical position of the Autonomous Territories, Autonomous Republics and Allied Republics in the Constitution of the Union and having granted in full the right of nations to self-determination—the dictatorship of the proletariat in the U.S.S.R., by this guarantees, not only formal, but also real equality for the different nationalities of the Union.

Being the land of the dictatorship of the proletariat and of Socialist construction, the land of great working class achievements, of the union of the workers with the peasants and of a new culture marching under the banner of Marxism —the U.S.S.R. inevitably becomes the base of the world movement of all oppressed classes, the center of international revolution, the greatest factor in world history. In the U.S.S.R., the world proletariat for the first time acquires a country that is really its own, and for the colonial movements the U.S.S.R. becomes a powerful center of attraction.

Thus, the U.S.S.R. is an extremely important factor in the general crisis of capitalism, not only because she has dropped out of the world capitalist system and has created a basis for a new Socialist system of production, but also because she plays an exceptionally great revolutionary role generally; she is the international driving force of proletarian revolution that impels the proletariat of all countries to seize power; she is the living example proving that the working class is not only capable of destroying capitalism, but of building up Socialism as well; she is the prototype of the fraternity of nationalities in all lands united in the World Union of Socialist Republics and of the economic unity of the toilers of all countries in a single world Socialist economic system that the world proletariat must establish when it has captured political power.

The simultaneous existence of two economic systems: the Socialist system in the U.S.S.R. and the capitalist system in other countries, imposes on the Proletarian State the task of warding off the blows showered upon it by the capitalist world (boycott, blockade, etc.), and also compels it to resort to economic maneuvering with and utilizing economic contacts with capitalist countries (with the aid of the monopoly of foreign trade—which is one of the fundamental conditions for the successful building up of Socialism, and also with the aid of credits, loans, concessions, etc.). The principal and fundamental line to be followed in this connection must be the line of establishing the widest possible contact with foreign countries—within limits determined by their usefulness to the U.S.S.R., i. e. primarily for strengthening industry in the U.S.S.R., for laying the base for her own heavy industry and electrification and finally, for the development of her own Socialist engineering industry. Only to the extent that the economic independence of the U.S.S.R., in the capitalist environment is secured can solid guarantees be obtained against the danger that Socialist construction in the U.S.S.R. may be destroyed and that the U.S.S.R. may be transformed into an appendage of the world capitalist system.

On the other hand, notwithstanding their interest in the markets of the U.S.S.R., the capitalist States continually vacillate between their commercial interests and their fear of the growth of the U.S.S.R., which means the growth of international revolution. However, the principal and fundamental tendency in the policy of the imperialist Powers is to encircle the U.S.S.R. and conduct counter-revolutionary war against her in order to strangle her and to establish a world bourgeois terrorist régime.

The systematic imperialist attempts politically to encircle the U.S.S.R. and the growing danger of an armed attack upon her, do not, however, prevent the Communist Party of the Soviet Union—a section of the Communist International and the leader of the proletarian dictatorship in the U.S.S.R.—from fulfilling its international obligations and from rendering support to all the oppressed, to the labor movements in capitalist countries, to colonial movements against imperialism and to the struggle against national oppression in every form.

3. The Duties of the International Proletariat to the U.S.S.R.

In view of the fact that the U.S.S.R. is the only father-land of the international proletariat, the principal bulwark of its achievements and the most important factor for its international emancipation, the international proletariat must on its part facilitate the success of the work of Social-ist construction in the U.S.S.R. and defend her against the attacks of the capitalist powers by all the means in its power.

"The world political situation has made the dicta-torship of the proletariat an immediate issue, and all the events of world politics are inevitably concentrat-ing around one central point, namely, the struggle of the world bourgeoisie against the Soviet Russian Re-public, which must inevitably group around itself the Soviet movements of the advanced workers of all coun-tries on the one hand, and all the national liberation

222

movements of the colonial and oppressed nationalities on the other." *(Lenin)*

In the event of the imperialist States declaring war upon and attacking the U.S.S.R., the international proletariat must retaliate by organizing bold and determined mass action and struggle for the overthrow of the imperialist governments with the solgan of: Dictatorship of the proletariat and alliance with the U.S.S.R.

In the colonies, and particularly the colonies of the imperialist country attacking the U.S.S.R., every effort must be made to take advantage of the diversion of the imperialist military forces to develop an anti-imperialist struggle and to organize revolutionary action for the purpose of throwing off the yoke of imperialism and of winning complete independence.

The development of Socialism in the U.S.S.R. and the growth of its international influence not only rouse the hatred of the capitalist States and their Social-Democratic agents against her, but also inspire the toilers all over the world with sympathy towards her and stimulate the readiness of the oppressed classes of all countries to fight with all the means in their power for the land of the proletarian dictatorship, in the event of an imperialist attack upon her.

Thus, the development of the contradictions within modern world economy, the development of the general capitalist crisis, and the imperialist military attack upon the Soviet Union inevitably lead to a mighty revolutionary outbreak which must overwhelm capitalism in a number of the so-called civilized countries, unleash the victorious revolution in the colonies, broaden the base of the proletarian dictatorship to an enormous degree and thus, with tremendous strides, bring nearer the final world victory of Socialism.

223

VI

THE STRATEGY AND TACTICS
OF THE COMMUNIST INTERNATIONAL
IN THE STRUGGLE
FOR THE DICTATORSHIP
OF THE PROLETARIAT

1. *Ideologies Among the Working Class Inimical to Communism*

I N ITS FIGHT AGAINST CAPITALISM for the dictatorship of the proletariat, revolutionary Communism encounters numerous tendencies among the working class, which to a more or less degree express the ideological subordination of the proletariat to the imperialist bourgeoisie, or reflect the ideological influence exercised upon the proletariat by the petty-bourgeoisie, which at times rebels against the shackles of finance capital, but is incapable of adopting sustained and scientifically planned strategy and tactics or of carrying on the struggle in an organized manner on the basis of the stern discipline that is characteristic of the proletariat.

The mighty social power of the imperialist State, with its auxiliary apparatus—schools, press, theatre and church—is primarily reflected in the existence of confessional and reformist tendencies among the working class, which represent the main obstacles on the road towards the proletarian social revolution.

The Confessional, religiously tinged tendency among the working class finds expression in the confessional trade

224

unions, which frequently are directly connected with corresponding bourgeois political organizations, and are affiliated to one or other of the church organizations of the dominant class (Catholic trade unions, Young Men's Christian Association, Jewish Zionist organizations, etc.). All these tendencies, being the most striking product of the ideological captivity of certain strata of the proletariat, in most cases, bear a romantic feudal tinge. By sanctifying all the abominations of the capitalist régime with the holy water of religion, and by terrorizing their flock with the specter of punishment in the world to come, the leaders of these organizations serve as the most reactionary units of the class enemy in the camp of the proletariat.

A cynically commercial, and imperialistic secular form of subjecting the proletariat to the ideological influence of the bourgeoisie is represented by contemporary "socialist" reformism. Taking its main gospel from the tablets of imperialist politics, its model today is the deliberately anti-socialist and openly counter-revolutionary "American Federation of Labor." The "ideological" dictatorship of the servile American trade union bureaucracy, which in its turn expresses the "ideological" dictatorship of the American dollar, has become, through the medium of British reformism and His Majesty's Socialists of the British Labor Party, the most important constituent in the theory and practice of international Social Democracy and of the leaders of the Amsterdam International, while the leaders of German and Austrian Social Democracy embellish these theories with Marxian phraseology in order to cover up their utter betrayal of Marxism. "Socialist" reformism, the principal enemy of revolutionary Communism in the labor movement, which has a broad organizational base in the Social Democratic parties and through these in the reformist trade

225

unions, in its entire policy and theoretical outlook stands out as a force directed against the proletarian revolution.

In the sphere of foreign politics, the Social Democratic parties actively supported the imperialist war on the pretext of "defending the fatherland." Imperialist expansion and "colonial policy" received their wholehearted support. Orientation towards the counter-revolutionary "Holy Alliance" of imperialist Powers ("The League of Nations"), advocacy of "ultra-imperialism," mobilization of the masses under pseudo-pacifist slogans, and at the same time, active support of imperialism in its attacks upon the U.S.S.R. and in the impending war against the U.S.S.R.—are the main features of reformist foreign policy.

In the sphere of home politics, Social Democracy has set itself the task of directly cooperating with and supporting the capitalist régime. Complete support for capitalist rationalization and stabilization, class peace, "peace in industry"; the policy of converting the labor organizations into organizations of the employers and of the predatory imperialist State; the practice of so-called "industrial democracy" which in fact means complete subordination to trustified capital; adoration of the imperialist State and particularly of its false democratic labels; active participation in the building up of the organs of the imperialist State—police, army, gendarmerie, its class judiciary; the defense of the State against the encroachments of the revolutionary Communist proletariat and the executioner's role Social Democracy plays in time of revolutionary crisis—such is the line of reformist home policy. While pretending to conduct the industrial struggle, reformism considers its function in this field to be to conduct that struggle in such a manner as to guard the capitalist class against any kind of shock, or at all events, to preserve the complete inviolability of the foundations of capitalist property.

In the sphere of theory, Social Democracy has utterly and completely betrayed Marxism, having traversed the road from revisionism to complete liberal bourgeois reformism and avowed social-imperialism: it has substituted in place of the Marxian theory of the contradictions of capitalism, the bourgeois theory of its harmonious development; it has pigeonholed the theory of crisis and of the pauperization of the proletariat; it has turned the flaming and menacing theory of class struggle into prosaic advocacy of class peace; it has exchanged the theory of growing class antagonisms for the petty-bourgeois fairy-tale about the "democratization" of capital; in place of the theory of the inevitability of war under capitalism it has substituted the bourgeois deceit of pacifism and the lying propaganda of "ultra-imperialism"; it has exchanged the theory of the revolutionary downfall of capitalism for the counterfeit coinage of "sound" capitalism transforming itself peacefully into Socialism; it has replaced revolution by evolution, the destruction of the bourgeois State by its active upbuilding, the theory of proletarian dictatorship by the theory of coalition with the bourgeoisie, the doctrine of international proletarian solidarity—by preaching defense of the imperialist fatherland; for Marxian dialectical materialism it has substituted the idealist philosophy and is now engaged in picking up the crumbs of religion that fall from the table of the bourgeoisie.

Within Social Democratic reformism a number of tendencies stand out that are characteristic of the bourgeois degeneracy of the Social Democracy.

Constructive Socialism (MacDonald & Co.), which, by its very name suggests the struggle against the revolutionary proletariat and a favorable attitude towards the capitalist system, continues the liberal philanthropic, anti-revolutionary and bourgeois traditions of Fabianism (Beatrice and Sydney Webb, Bernard Shaw, Lord Oliver, etc.). While repudiating the dictatorship of the proletariat and the use of violence in the struggle against the bourgeoisie as a matter of principle, it favors violence in the struggle against the proletariat and the colonial peoples. While acting as the apologists of the capitalist State and preaching State capitalism under the guise of Socialism, and, in conjunction with the most vulgar ideologists of imperialism in both hemispheres, declaring the theory of the class struggle to be a "pre-scientific" theory, "Constructive Socialism" ostensibly advocates a moderate program of nationalization with compensation, taxation of land values, death duties, and taxation of surplus profits as a means for abolishing capitalism. Being resolutely opposed to the dictatorship of the proletariat in the U.S.S.R., "Constructive Socialism," in complete alliance with the bourgeoisie—is an active enemy of the Communist proletarian movement and of colonial revolutions.

A special variety of "Constructive Socialism" is "Co-operativism," or "Cooperative Socialism" (Charles Gide, Totomyanz & Co.), which also strongly repudiates the class struggle and advocates the cooperative organization of consumers as a means of overcoming capitalism, but which in fact does all it can to help the stabilization of capitalism. Having at its command an extensive propagandist apparatus, in the shape of the mass consumers' cooperative organizations, which it employs for the purpose of systematically influencing the masses, "Cooperativism" carries on a fierce struggle against the revolutionary labor movement, hampers it in the achievement of its aims and represents today one of the most potent factors in the camp of the reformist counter-revolution.

So-called "Guild Socialism" (Penty, Orage, Hobson and others) is an eclectic attempt to unite "revolutionary" syndicalism with bourgeois liberal Fabianism, anarchist decentralization ("national industrial guilds") with State capitalist centralization and mediaeval guild and craft narrowness with modern capitalism. Starting out with the ostensible demand for the abolition of the "wage system" as an "immoral" institution which must be abolished by means of workers' control of industry, Guild Socialism completely ignores the most important question, viz., the question of power. While striving to unite workers, intellectuals, and technicians into a federation of national industrial "guilds" and to convert these guilds by peaceful means ("control from within") into organs for the administration of industry within the framework of the bourgeois State, Guild Socialism actually defends the bourgeois State, obscures its class, imperialist and anti-proletarian character and allots to it the function of the non-class representative of the interests of the "consumers" as against the guild organized "producers." By its advocacy of "functional democracy," i.e., representation of classes in capitalist society— each class being presumed to have a definite social and productive function—Guild Socialism paves the way for the Fascist "Corporate State." By repudiating both parliamentarism and "direct action," the majority of the Guild Socialists doom the working class to inaction and passive subordination to the bourgeoisie. Thus, Guild Socialism represents a peculiar form of trade unionist utopian opportunism and, as such, cannot but play an anti-revolutionary role.

Lastly, Austro-Marxism represents a special variety of Social Democratic reformism. Being a part of the "Left-wing" of Social Democracy, Austro-Marxism represents a most subtle deception of the masses of the toilers. Prostituting the terminology of Marxism, while divorcing themselves entirely from the principles of revolutionary Marxism (the Kantism, Machism, etc., of the Austro-Marxists in the domain of philosophy), toying with religion, borrowing the theory of "functional democracy" from the British reformists, agreeing with the principle of "building up the Republic," i.e. building up the bourgeois State, Austro-Marxism recommends "class cooperation" in periods of so-called "equilibrium of class forces," i.e. precisely at the time when the revolutionary crisis is maturing. This theory is a justification of coalition with the bourgeoisie for the overthrow of the proletarian revolution under the guise of defending "democracy" against the attacks of reaction. Objectively, and in practice, the violence which Austro-Marxism admits in cases of reactionary attacks is converted into reactionary violence against the proletarian revolution. Hence, the "functional role" of Austro-Marxism is to deceive the workers already marching towards Communism, and therefore, it is the most dangerous enemy of the proletariat, more dangerous than the avowed adherents of predatory social imperialism.

All the above-mentioned tendencies, being constituent parts of "Socialist" reformism, are agencies of the imperialist bourgeoisie within the working class itself. But Communism has to contend also against a number of petty-bourgeois tendencies, which reflect and express the vacillation of the unstable strata of society (the urban petty-bourgeoisie, the degenerate city middle class, the slum proletariat, the declassed Bohemian intellectuals, the pauperized artisans, certain strata of the peasantry, etc., etc.). These tendencies, which are distinguished for their extreme political instability, often cover up a Right wing policy with Left wing phraseology or drop into adventurism, substitute noisy political gesticulation for objective estimation of forces and often tumble from astounding heights of revolutionary bombast to profound depths of pessimism and downright capitulation before the enemy. Under certain conditions, particularly in periods of sharp changes in the political situation and of forced temporary retreat, these tendencies may become very dangerous disrupters of the proletarian ranks and consequently, a drag upon the revolutionary proletarian movement.

Anarchism, the most prominent representatives of which (Kropotkin, Jean Graves and others) treacherously went over to the side of the imperialist bourgeoisie in the war of 1914-1918, denies the necessity for wide, centralized and disciplined proletarian organizations and thus leaves the proletariat powerless before the powerful organizations of capital. By its advocacy of individual terror, it distracts the proletariat from the methods of mass organization and mass struggle. By repudiating the dictatorship of the proletariat in the name of "abstract" liberty, anarchism deprives the proletariat of its most important and sharpest weapon against the bourgeoisie, its armies, and all its organs of repression. Being remote from mass movements of any kind in the most important centers of proletarian struggle, Anarchism is steadily being reduced to a sect which, by its tactics and actions, including its opposition to the dictatorship of the working class in the U.S.S.R., has objectively joined the united front of the anti-revolutionary forces.

"Revolutionary" Syndicalism, many ideologists of which, in the extremely critical war period went over to the camp of the Fascist type of "anti-parliamentary" counter-revolutionaries, or became peaceful reformists of the Social Democratic type, by its repudiation of political struggle (particularly of revolutionary parliamentarism) and of the revolutionary dictatorship of the proletariat, by its advocacy of the craft decentralization of the labor movement generally and of the trade union movement in particular, by its repudiation of the need for a proletarian party, and of the necessity for rebellion, and by its exaggeration of the importance of the general strike (the "fold arm tactics"), like Anarchism, hinders the revolutionization of the masses of the workers wherever it has any influence. Its attacks upon the U.S.S.R., which logically follow from its repudiation of dictatorship of the proletariat in general, place it in this respect on a level with Social Democracy.

All these tendencies take a common stand with Social Democracy, the principal enemy of the proletarian revolution, on the fundamental political issue, viz., the question of the Dictatorship of the Proletariat. Hence, all of them come out more or less definitely in a united front with Social Democracy against the U.S.S.R. On the other hand, Social Democracy, which has utterly and completely betrayed Marxism, tends to rely more and more upon the ideology of the Fabians, of the Constructive Socialists and of the Guild Socialists. These tendencies are becoming transformed into the official liberal-reformist ideology of the bourgeois "Socialism" of the Second International.

In the colonial countries and among the oppressed peoples and races generally, Communism encounters the influence of peculiar tendencies in the labor movement which played a useful role in a definite phase of development, but which, in the new stage of development, are becoming transformed into a reactionary force.

Sun Yat-senism in China expressed the ideology of petty-bourgeois democratic "Socialism." In the "Three Principles" (nationalism, democracy, Socialism), the concept "people" obscured the concept "classes"; Socialism was presented, not as a specific mode of production to be carried on by a specific class, i.e. by the proletariat, but as a vague state of social well-being, while no connection was made between the struggle against imperialism and the perspectives of the development of the class struggle. Therefore, while it played a very useful role in the first stage of the Chinese Revolution, as a consequence of the further process of class differentiation that has taken place in the country and of the further progress of the revolution, Sun Yat-senism has now changed from being the ideological expression of the development of that revolution into fetters of its further development. The epigones of Sun Yat-senism, by emphasizing and exaggerating the very features of this ideology that have become objectively reactionary, have made it the official ideology of the Kuomintang, which is now an openly counter-revolutionary force. The ideological growth of the masses of the Chinese proletariat and of the toiling peasantry must therefore be accompanied by determined decisive struggle against the Kuomintang deception and by opposition to the remnants of the Sun Yat-senist ideology.

Tendencies like Gandhi-ism in India, thoroughly imbued with religious conceptions, idealize the most backward and economically most reactionary forms of social life, see the solution of the social problem not in proletarian Socialism, but in a reversion to these backward forms, preach passivity and repudiate the class struggle, and in the process of the development of the revolution become transformed into an openly reactionary force. Gandhi-ism is more and more becoming an ideology directed against mass revolution. It must be strongly combated by Communism.

Garveyism, which formerly was the ideology of the Negro small property owners and workers in America, and which even now exercises some influence over the Negro masses, like Gandhi-ism, has become a hindrance to the revolutionization of the Negro masses. Originally advocating social equality for Negroes, Garveyism subsequently developed into a peculiar form of Negro "Zionism" which, instead of fighting American imperialism, advanced the slogan: "Back to Africa"! This dangerous ideology, which bears not a single genuine democratic trait, and which toys with the aristocratic attributes of a non-existent "Negro kingdom," must be strongly resisted, for it is not a help but a hindrance to the mass Negro struggle for liberation against American imperialism.

Standing out against all these tendencies is Proletarian Communism. The powerful ideology of the international revolutionary working class, it differs from all these tendencies, and primarily from Social Democracy, in that, in complete harmony with the teachings of Marx and Engels, it conducts a theoretical and practical revolutionary struggle for the Dictatorship of the Proletariat, and in the struggle applies all forms of proletarian mass action.

2. The Fundamental Tasks
of Communist Strategy and Tactics

The successful struggle of the Communist International for the dictatorship of the proletariat presupposes the existence in every country of a compact Communist Party, hardened in the struggle, disciplined, centralized, and closely linked up with the masses.

The Party is the vanguard of the working class and consists of the best, most class-conscious, most active, and most

234

courageous members of that class. It incorporates the whole body of experience of the proletarian struggle. Basing itself upon the revolutionary theory of Marxism and representing the general and lasting interests of the whole of the working class, the Party personifies the unity of proletarian principles, of proletarian will and of proletarian revolutionary action. It is a revolutionary organization, bound by iron discipline and strict revolutionary rules of democratic centralism, which can be carried out thanks to the class-consciousness of the proletarian vanguard, to its loyalty to the revolution, its ability to maintain inseparable ties with the proletarian masses and to its correct political leadership, which is constantly verified and clarified by the experiences of the masses themselves.

In order that it may fulfill its historic mission of achieving the dictatorship of the proletariat, the Communist Party must first of all set itself and accomplish the following fundamental strategic aims:

Extend its influence over the majority of the members of its own class, including working women and the working youth. To achieve this the Communist Party must secure predominant influence in the broad mass proletarian organizations (Soviets, trade unions, factory councils, cooperative societies, sport organizations, cultural organizations, etc.). It is particularly important for the purpose of winning over the majority of the proletariat, to capture the trade unions, which are genuine mass working-class organizations closely bound up with the everyday struggles of the working class. To work in reactionary trade unions and skillfully to capture them, to win the confidence of the broad masses of the industrially organized workers, to change and "remove from their posts" the reformist leaders, represent important tasks in the preparatory period.

235

The achievement of the dictatorship of the proletariat presupposes also that the proletariat acquires hegemony over wide sections of the toiling masses. To accomplish this the Communist Party must extend its influence over the masses of the urban and rural poor, over the lower strata of the intelligentsia and over the so-called "small man," i.e. the petty-bourgeois strata generally. It is particularly important that work be carried on for the purpose of extending the Party's influence over the peasantry. The Communist Party must secure for itself the whole-hearted support of that stratum of the rural population that stands closest to the proletariat, i.e. the agricultural laborers and the rural poor. To this end, the agricultural laborers must be organized in separate organizations; all possible support must be given them in their struggles against the rural bourgeoisie, and strenuous work must be carried on among the small allotment farmers and small peasants. In regard to the middle strata of the peasantry in developed capitalist countries, the Communist Parties must conduct a policy to secure their neutrality. The fulfillment of all these tasks by the proletariat—the champion of the interests of the whole people and the leader of the broad masses in their struggle against the oppression of finance capital—is an essential condition precedent for the victorious Communist revolution.

The tasks of the Communist International connected with the revolutionary struggle in colonies, semi-colonies and dependencies are extremely important strategical tasks in the world proletarian struggle. The colonial struggle presupposes that the broad masses of the working class and of the peasantry in the colonies be rallied round the banner of the revolution; but this cannot be achieved unless the closest cooperation is maintained between the proletariat in the oppressing countries and the toiling masses in the oppressed countries.

While organizing, under the banner of the proletarian dictatorship, the revolution against imperialism in the so-called civilized States, the Communist International supports every movement against imperialist violence in the colonies, semi-colonies and dependencies themselves (for example Latin-America); it carries on propaganda against all forms of chauvinism and against the imperialist mal-treatment of enslaved peoples and races, big and small (treatment of Negroes, "yellow labor," anti-semitism, etc.) and supports their struggles against the bourgeoisie of the oppressing nations. The Communist International especially combats the chauvinism that is preached in the Empire-owning countries by the imperialist bourgeoise as well as by its Social-Democratic agency, the Second International, and constantly holds up in contrast to the practices of the imperialist bourgeoisie the practice of the Soviet Union, which has established relations of fraternity and equality among the nationalities inhabiting it.

The Communist Parties in the imperialist countries must render systematic aid to the colonial revolutionary liberation movement and to the movement of oppressed nationalities generally. The duty of rendering active support to these movements rests primarily upon the workers in the countries upon which the oppressed nations are economically, financially or politically dependent. The Communist Parties must openly recognize the right of the colonies to separation and their right to carry on propaganda for this separation, i.e. propaganda in favor of the independence of the colonies from the imperialist State; they must recognize their right of armed defense against imperialism (i.e. the right of rebellion and revolutionary war) and advocate and give active support to this defense by all the means in their power. The Communist Parties must adopt this line of policy in regard to all oppressed nations.

The Communist Parties in the colonial and semi-colonial countries must carry on a bold and consistent struggle against foreign imperialism and unfailingly conduct propaganda in favor of friendship and unity with the proletariat in the imperialist countries. They must openly advance, conduct propaganda for and carry out the slogan of agrarian revolution, rouse the broad masses of the peasantry for the overthrow of the landlords and combat the reactionary and mediaeval influence of the clergy, of the missionaries and other similar elements.

In these countries, the principal task is to organize the workers and the peasantry independently (to establish class Communist Parties of the proletariat, trade unions, peasant leagues and committees and, in a revolutionary situation, Soviets, etc.) and to free them from the influence of the national bourgeoisie, with whom temporary agreements may be made only on the condition that they, the bourgeoisie, do not hamper the revolutionary organization of the workers and peasants, and that they carry on a genuine struggle against imperialism.

In determining its line of tactics, each Communist Party must take into account the concrete internal and external situation, the correlation of class forces, the degree of stability and strength of the bourgeoisie, the degree of preparedness of the proletariat, the position taken up by the various intermediary strata in its country, etc. The Party determines its slogans and methods of struggle in accordance with these circumstances, with the view to organizing and mobilizing the masses on the broadest possible scale and on the highest possible level of this struggle.

When a revolutionary situation is developing, the Party advances certain transitional slogans and partial demands corresponding to the concrete situation; but these demands and slogans must be bent to the revolutionary aim of capturing power and of overthrowing bourgeois capitalist society. The Party must neither stand aloof from the daily needs and struggles of the working class nor confine its activities exclusively to them. The task of the Party is to utilize these minor every-day needs as a starting point from which to lead the working class to the revolutionary struggle for power.

When the revolutionary tide is rising, when the ruling classes are disorganized, the masses are in a state of revolutionary ferment, the intermediary strata are inclining towards the proletariat and the masses are ready for action and for sacrifice, the Party of the proletariat is confronted with the task of leading the masses to a direct attack upon the bourgeois State. This it does by carrying on propaganda in favor of increasingly radical transitional slogans (for Soviets, workers' control of industry, for peasant committees for the seizure of the big landed properties, for disarming the bourgeoisie and arming the proletariat, etc.) and by organizing mass action, upon which all branches of Party agitation and propaganda, including parliamentary activity, must be concentrated. This mass action includes: a combination of strikes and demonstrations; a combination of strikes and armed demonstrations; and finally, the general strike conjointly with armed insurrection against the State power of the bourgeoisie. The latter form of struggle, which is the supreme form, must be conducted according to the rules of war; it presupposes a plan of campaign, offensive fighting operations and unbounded devotion and heroism on the part of the proletariat. An absolutely essential condition precedent for this form of action is the organization of the broad masses into militant units, which, by their very form, embrace and set into action the largest possible numbers of toilers (Councils of Workers' Deputies, Soldiers' Councils, etc.), and intensified revolutionary work in the army and the navy.

In passing over to new and more radical slogans, the Parties must be guided by the fundamental role of the political tactics of Leninism, which call for ability to lead the masses to revolutionary positions in such a manner that the masses may, by their own experience, convince themselves of the correctness of the Party line. Failure to observe this rule must inevitably lead to isolation from the masses, to putschism, to the ideological degeneration of Communism into "Leftist" dogmatism and to petty-bourgeois "revolutionary" adventurism. Failure to take advantage of the culminating point in the development of the revolutionary situation, when the Party of the proletariat is called upon to conduct a bold and determined attack upon the enemy, is not less dangerous. To allow that opportunity to slip by and to fail to start rebellion at that point, means to allow the initiative to pass to the enemy and to doom the revolution to defeat.

When the revolutionary tide is not rising, the Communist Parties must advance partial slogans and demands that correspond to the every day needs of the toilers, and combine them with the fundamental tasks of the Communist International. The Communist Parties must not, however, at such a time, advance transitional slogans that are applicable only to revolutionary situations (for example workers' control of industry, etc.). To advance such slogans when there is no revolutionary situation means to transform them into slogans that favor merging with the capitalist system of organization. Partial demands and slogans generally form an essential part of correct tactics; but certain transitional slogans go inseparably with a revolutionary situation. Repudiation of partial demands and transitional slogans "on principle," however, is incompatible with the tactical principles of Communism, for in effect, such repudiation condemns the Party to inaction and isolates it from the masses. United front tactics also occupy an important place in the tactics of the Communist Parties throughout the whole pre-revolutionary period as a means towards achieving success in the struggle against capital, towards the class mobilization of the masses and the exposure and isolation of the reformist leaders.

The correct application of united front tactics and the fulfillment of the general task of winning over the masses presuppose in their turn systematic and persistent work in the trade unions and other mass proletarian organizations. It is the bounden duty of every Communist to belong to a trade union, even a most reactionary one, provided it is a mass organization. Only by constant and persistent work in the trade unions and in the factories for the steadfast and energetic defense of the interests of the workers, together with ruthless struggle against the reformist bureaucracy, will it be possible to win the leadership in the workers' struggle and to win the industrially organized workers over to the side of the Party.

Unlike the reformists, whose policy is to split the trade unions, the Communists defend trade union unity nationally and internationally on the basis of the class struggle, and render every support to and strengthen the work of the Red International of Labor Unions.

In universally championing the current every day needs of the masses of the workers and of the toilers generally, in

241

utilizing the bourgeois parliament as a platform for revolutionary agitation and propaganda, and subordinating the partial tasks to the struggle for the dictatorship of the proletariat, the Parties of the Communist International advance partial demands and slogans in the following main spheres:

In the sphere of Labor, in the narrow meaning of the term, i.e. questions concerned with the industrial struggle (the fight against the trustified capitalist offensive, wages questions, the working day, compulsory arbitration, unemployment), which grow into questions of the general political struggle (big industrial conflicts, fight for the right to organize, right to strike, etc.); in the sphere of politics proper (taxation, high cost of living, Fascism, persecution of revolutionary parties, white terror and current politics generally); and finally the sphere of world politics, viz., attitude towards the U.S.S.R. and colonial revolutions, struggle for the unity of the international trade union movement, struggle against imperialism and the war danger, and systematic preparation for the fight against imperialist war.

In the sphere of the peasant problem, the partial demands are those appertaining to taxation, peasant mortgage indebtedness, struggle against usurer's capital, the land hunger of the peasant small holders, rent, the metayer (crop-sharing) system. Starting out from these partial needs, the Communist Party must sharpen the respective slogans and broaden them out into the slogans: confiscation of large estates, and workers' and peasants' government (the synonym for proletarian dictatorship in developed capitalist countries and for democratic dictatorship of the proletariat and peasantry in backward countries and in certain colonies).

Systematic work must also be carried on among the proletarian and peasant youth (mainly through the Young Com-

munist International and its Sections) and also among
working women and peasant women. This work must con-
cern itself with the special conditions of life and struggle
of the working and peasant women, and their demands
must be linked up with the general demands and fighting
slogans of the proletariat.

In the struggle against colonial oppression, the Communist Parties in the colonies must advance partial demands that correspond to the special circumstances prevailing in each country such as: complete equality for all
nations and races; abolition of all privileges for foreigners;
the right of association for workers and peasants; reduction
of the working day; prohibition of child labor; prohibition
of usury and of all transactions entailing bondage; reduction and abolition of rent; reduction of taxation; refusal to
pay taxes, etc. All these partial slogans must be subordinate
to the fundamental demands of the Communist Parties
such as: complete political national independence and the
expulsion of the imperialists; workers' and peasants' government, the land to the whole people, eight-hour day, etc. The
Communist Parties in imperialist countries, while supporting the struggle proceeding in the colonies, must carry on
a campaign in their own respective countries for the withdrawal of imperialist troops, conduct propaganda in the
army and navy in defense of the oppressed countries fighting for their liberation, mobilize the masses to refuse to
transport troops and munitions and, in connection with
this, to organize strikes and other forms of mass protest, etc.

The Communist International must devote itself especially to systematic preparation for the struggle against the
danger of imperialist wars. Ruthless exposure of social
chauvinism, of social imperialism and of pacifist phrase-
mongering intended to camouflage the imperialist plans of

the bourgeoisie; propaganda in favor of the principal slogans of the Communist International; every day organizational work in connection with this, in the course of which work legal methods must unfailingly be combined with illegal methods; organized work in the army and navy—such must be the activity of the Communist Parties in this connection. The fundamental slogans of the Communist International in this connection must be the following: Convert imperialist war into civil war; defeat the "home" imperialist government; defend the U.S.S.R. and the colonies by every possible means in the event of imperialist war against them. It is the bounden duty of all Sections of the Communist International, and of every one of its members, to carry on propaganda for these slogans, to expose the "Socialistic" sophisms and the "Socialistic" camouflage of the League of Nations and constantly to keep to the front the experiences of the war of 1914-1918.

In order that revolutionary work and revolutionary action may be coordinated and in order that these activities may be guided most successfully, the international proletariat must be bound by international class discipline, for which, first of all, it is most important to have the strictest international discipline in the Communist ranks.

This international Communist discipline must find expression in the subordination of the partial and local interests of the movement to its general and lasting interests and in the strict fulfillment, by all members, of the decisions passed by the leading bodies of the Communist International.

Unlike the Social-Democratic, Second International, each section of which submits to the discipline of "its own" national bourgeoisie and of its own "fatherland," the sections of the Communist International submit to only one discipline, viz., international proletarian discipline, which guarantees victory in the struggle of the world's workers for world proletarian dictatorship. Unlike the Second International, which splits the trade unions, fights against colonial peoples, and practices unity with the bourgeoisie, the Communist International is an organization that guards proletarian unity in all countries and the unity of the toilers of all races and all peoples in their struggle against the yoke of imperialism.

Despite the bloody terror of the bourgeoisie, the Communists fight with courage and devotion on all sectors of the international class front, in the firm conviction that the victory of the proletariat is inevitable and cannot be averted.

"The Communists disdain to conceal their views and aims. They openly declare that their aims can be attained only by the forcible overthrow of all the existing social conditions. Let the ruling class tremble at a Communist revolution. The proletarians have nothing to lose but their chains. They have a world to win.

"Workers of all countries, unite!"

PART 4

CONSTITUTION AND RULES
OF THE COMMUNIST INTERNATIONAL

CONSTITUTION AND RULES
OF THE COMMUNIST INTERNATIONAL

I. Name and Objects

THE COMMUNIST INTERNATIONAL—the International Workers' Association—is a union of Communist Parties in various countries; it it a World Communist Party. As the leader and organizer of the world revolutionary movement of the proletariat and the bearer of the principles and aims of Communism, the Communist International strives to win over the majority of the working class and the broad strata of the propertyless peasantry, fights for the establishment of the world dictatorship of the proletariat, for the establishment of a World Union of Socialist Soviet Republics, for the complete abolition of classes and for the achievement of Socialism—the first stage of Communist society.

2. The various Parties affiliated to the Communist International are called the Communist Party of——————— [name of country] (Section of the Communist International). In any given country there can be only one Communist Party affiliated to the Communist International and representing its Section in that country.

3. Membership of the Communist Party and of the Communist International is open to all those who accept the program and rules of the given Communist Party and of the Communist International, who join one of the basic units of a Party, actively work in it, abide by all the decisions of the Party and of the Communist International, and regu-

larly pay Party dues.

4. The basic unit of the Communist Party organization is the nucleus in the place of employment (factory, workshop, mine, office, store, farm, etc.) which unites all the Party members employed in the given enterprise.

5. The Communist International and its Sections are built up on the basis of democratic centralism, the fundamental principles of which are: (a) election of all the leading committees of the Party, subordinate and superior (by general meetings of Party members, conferences, congresses and international congresses); (b) periodical reports by leading Party committees to their constituents; (c) decisions of superior Party committees to be obligatory for subordinate committees, strict Party discipline and prompt execution of the decisions of the Communist International, of its leading committees and of the leading Party organs.

Party questions may be discussed by the members of the Party and by Party organizations until such time as a decision is taken upon them by the competent Party committees. After a decision has been taken by the Congress of the Communist International, by the Congress of the respective Sections, or by leading committees of the Comintern, and of its various Sections, these decisions must be unreservedly carried out even if a Section of the Party membership or of the local Party organizations are in disagreement with it.

In cases where a Party exists illegally, the superior Party committees may appoint the subordinate committees and coopt members on their own committees, subject to subsequent endorsement by the competent superior Party committees.

6. In all non-Party workers' and peasants' mass organizations and in their leading committees (trade unions, co-

operative societies, sport organizations, ex-service men's organizations, and at their congresses and conferences) and also on municipal bodies and in parliament, even if there are only two Party members in such organizations and bodies, Communist fractions must be formed for the purpose of strengthening the Party's influence and for carrying out its policy in these organizations and bodies.

7. The Communist fractions are subordinated to the competent Party bodies.

NOTE: 1. Communist fractions in international organizations (Red International of Labor Unions, International Class War Prisoners' Aid Society, International Workers Relief, etc.) are subordinate to the Executive Committee of the Communist International.

2. The organizational structure of the Communist fractions and the manner in which their work is guided are determined by special instructions from the Executive Committee of the Communist International and from the Central Committees of the given Sections of the Comintern.

II.   The World Congress of the Communist International

8. The supreme body of the Communist International is the World Congress of representatives of all Parties (Sections) and organizations affiliated to the Communist International.

The World Congress discusses and decides program, tactical and organizational questions connected with the activities of the Communist International and of its various Sections. Power to alter the program and rules of the Communist International lies exclusively with the World Congress of the Communist International.

The World Congress shall be convened once every two years. The date of the Congress and the number of representatives from the various Sections to the Congress to be determined by the Executive Committee of the Communist International.

The number of decisive votes to be allocated to each Section at the World Congress shall be determined by a special decision of the Congress itself, in accordance with the membership of the given Party and the political importance of the given country. Delegates to the Congress must have a free mandate; no imperative mandate can be recognized.

9. Special Congresses of the Communist International shall be convened on the demand of Parties which, at the preceding World Congress had an aggregate of not less than one half of the decisive votes.

10. The World Congress elects the Executive Committee of the Communist International (E.C.C.I.) and the International Control Commission (I.C.C.).

11. The headquarters of the Executive Committee is decided on by the World Congress.

III. *The Executive Committee of the Communist International and Its Subsidiary Bodies*

12. The leading body of the Communist International in the period between Congresses is the Executive Com-

mittee, which gives instructions to all the Sections of the Communist International and controls their activity.

The E.C.C.I. publishes the Central Organ of the Communist International, in not less than four languages.

13. The decisions of the E.C.C.I. are obligatory for all the Sections of the Communist International and must be promptly carried out. The Sections have the right to appeal against decisions of the E.C.C.I. to the World Congress, but must continue to carry out such decisions pending the decision of the World Congress.

14. The Central Committees of the various Sections of the Communist International are responsible to their respective Party Congress and to the E.C.C.I. The latter has the right to annul or amend decisions of Party Congresses and of Central Committees of Parties and also to make decisions which are obligatory for them. (Cf. Par. 13.)

15. The E.C.C.I. has the right to expel from the Communist International, entire Sections, groups and individual members who violate the program and rules of the Communist International or the decisions of the World Congress and of the E.C.C.I. Persons and bodies expelled have the right of appeal to the World Congress.

16. The programs of the various Sections of the Communist International must be endorsed by the E.C.C.I. In the event of the E.C.C.I. refusing to endorse a program, the Section concerned has the right to appeal to the World Congress of the Communist International.

17. The leading organs of the press of the various Sections of the Communist International must publish all the decisions and official documents of the E.C.C.I. These decisions must, as far as possible, be published also in the other organs of the Party press.

18. The E.C.C.I. has the right to accept affiliation to

the Communist International of organizations and Parties sympathetic to Communism, such organizations to have an advisory vote.

19. The E.C.C.I. elects a Presidium responsible to the E.C.C.I., which acts as the permanent body carrying out all the business of the E.C.C.I. in the interval between the meetings of the latter.

20. The E.C.C.I. and its Presidium have the right to establish permanent bureaus (Western European, South American, Eastern and other Bureaus of the E.C.C.I.) for the purpose of establishing closer contact with the various Sections of the Communist International and in order to be better able to guide their work.

NOTE: The scope of the activities of the permanent bureaus of the E.C.C.I. shall be determined by the E.C.C.I. or by its Presidium. The Sections of the Communist International which come within the scope of activities of the permanent bureaus of the E.C.C.I. must be informed by the powers conferred on these bureaus.

21. The Sections must carry out the instructions of the permanent bureaus of the E.C.C.I. Sections may appeal against the instructions of the permanent bureaus to the E.C.C.I. or to its Presidium, but must continue to carry out such instructions pending the decision of E.C.C.I. or of its Presidium.

22. The E.C.C.I. and its Presidium have the right to send their representatives to the various Sections of the Communist International. Such representatives receive their instructions from the E.C.C.I. or from its Presidium, and are responsible to them for their activities. Representatives of the E.C.C.I. have the right to participate in meetings of the central Party bodies as well as of the local organizations of

254

the Sections to which they are sent. Representatives of the E.C.C.I. must carry out their commission in close contact with the Central Committee of the Section to which they are sent. They may, however, speak in opposition to the Central Committee of the given Section, at Congresses and Conferences of that Section, if the line of the Central Committee in question diverges from the instructions of the E.C.C.I. Representatives of the E.C.C.I. are especially obliged to supervise the carrying out of the decisions of the World Congresses and of the Executive Committee of the Communist International.

The E.C.C.I. and its Presidium also have the right to send instructors to the various Sections of the Communist International. The powers and duties of instructors are determined by the E.C.C.I., to whom the instructors are responsible in their work.

23. Meetings of the E.C.C.I. must take place not less than once every six months. A quorum must consist of not less than one half of the membership of the E.C.C.I.

24. Meetings of the Presidium of the E.C.C.I. must take place not less than once a fortnight. A quorum must consist of not less than one half of the membership of the Presidium.

25. The Presidium elects the Political Secretariat, which is empowered to take decisions, and which also prepares questions for the meetings of the E.C.C.I. and of its Presidium, and acts as their executive body.

26. The Presidium appoints the editorial committees of the periodical and other publications of the Communist International.

27. The Presidium of the E.C.C.I. sets up a Department for Work Among Women Toilers, permanent committees for guiding the work of definite groups of Sections of the

255

Communist International (Lander Secretariats) and other departments necessary for its work.

IV. *The International Control Commission*

28. The International Control Commission investigates matters concerning the unity of the Sections affiliated to the Communist International and also matters connected with the Communist conduct of individual members of the various Sections.

For this purpose the I.C.C.:

a) Examines complaints against the actions of Central Committees of Communist Parties lodged by Party members who have been subjected to disciplinary measures for political differences;

b) Examines such analogous matters concerning members of central bodies of Communist Parties and of individual Party members as it deems necessary, or which are submitted to it by the deciding bodies of the E.C.C.I.;

c) Audits the accounts of the Communist International.

The International Control Commission must not intervene in the political differences or in organizational and administrative conflicts in the Communist Parties.

The headquarters of the I.C.C. are fixed by the I.C.C., in agreement with the E.C.C.I.

V. The Relationships
Between the Sections of the Communist International
and the E.C.C.I.

29. The Central Committees of Sections affiliated to the Communist International and the Central Committees of affiliated sympathizing organizations must send to the E.C.C.I. the Minutes of their meetings and reports of their work.

30. Resignation from office by individual members or groups of members of Central Committees of the various Sections are regarded as disruption of the Communist movement. Leading posts in the Party do not belong to the occupant of that post, but to the Communist International as a whole. Elected members of the Central leading bodies of the various Sections may resign, before their time of office expires, only with the consent of the E.C.C.I. Resignations accepted by Central Committees of Sections without the consent of the E.C.C.I. are invalid.

31. The Sections affiliated to the Communist International must maintain close organizational and informational contact with each other, arrange for mutual representation at each other's conferences and congresses, and, with the consent of the E.C.C.I., exchange leading comrades. This applies particularly to the Sections in imperial countries and their colonies, and to the Sections in countries adjacent to each other.

32. Two or more Sections of the Communist International which (like the Sections in the Scandinavian countries and in the Balkans) are politically connected with each other by common conditions of struggle, may, with the consent of the E.C.C.I., form federations for the purpose of

257

co-ordinating their activities, such federations to work under the guidance and control of the E.C.C.I.

33. The Sections of the Comintern must regularly pay affiliation dues to the E.C.C.I.; the amount of such dues to be determined by the E.C.C.I.

34. Congresses of the various Sections, ordinary and special, can be convened only with the consent of the E.C.C.I.

In the event of a Section failing to convene a Party Congress prior to the convening of a World Congress, that Section, before electing delegates to the World Congress, must convene a Party conference, or Plenum of its Central Committee, for the purpose of preparing the questions for the World Congress.

35. The Young Communist International is a Section of the Communist International with full rights and is subordinate to the E.C.C.I.

36. The Communist Parties must be prepared for transition to illegal conditions. The E.C.C.I. must render the Parties concerned assistance in their preparations for transition to illegal conditions.

37. Individual members of Sections of the Communist International may pass from one country to another only with the consent of the Central Committee of the Section of which they are members.

Communists changing their domicile must join the Section in the country of their new domicile. Communists leaving their country without the consent of the Central Committee of their Section, must not be accepted into other Sections of the Communist International.

INDEX

INDEX

The text of this book has been set in Electra, a linotype face designed by W. A. Dwiggins, with Weiss Initials. Typography by Monsen-Chicago, printing by George C. Melin and binding by the John F. Cuneo Company. Binding cloth, Atlas Impreglin, by Western Shade Cloth Company. Design by Rodney Chirpe.